Editorial project:
2021 © **booq** publishing, S.L.
c/ Domènech, 7-9, 2º 1ª
08012 Barcelona, Spain
T: +34 93 268 80 88
www.booqpublishing.com

ISBN: 978-84-9936-694-4 [EN]

© Editions du Layeur
Dépôt Légal : 2021
ISBN : 978-2-915126-97-6
Espagne, en juin 2021

monsa
publications

© 2021 Instituto Monsa de ediciones, S.L.
c/ Gravina, 43
08930 Sant Adrià de Besós, Barcelona, Spain
T: +34 93 381 00 93
www.monsa.com
monsa@monsa.com

ISBN: 978-84-17557-37-9

Editorial coordinator:
Claudia Martínez Alonso

Art director:
Mireia Casanovas Soley

Editor and layout:
David Andreu Bach

Translation:
© **booq** publishing, S.L.

Printing in Spain

ANDREAS BURGHARDT
NEUMEISTER WEINGUT
PHOTO © Andreas Burghardt

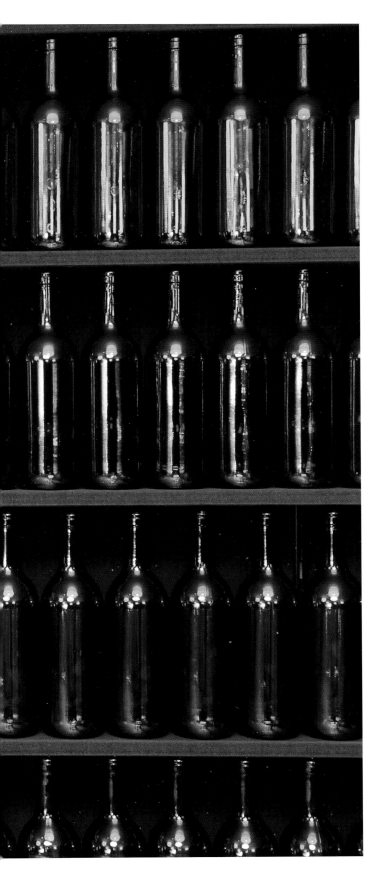

Although the architecture associated with the world of wine has experienced a real boom in the last ten years, as it seems that there is no major winery that does not have an interesting project, the truth is that even in the origins of the preparation of wine, great architectural works were carried out. For example, wine villages par excellence, such as Aranda de Duero or Langenlois (Austria), have kilometres of underground galleries to store their precious wines, dating back to the Middle Ages. Later came the famous Bordeaux producers and their magnificent chateaux - who were the first to recognise the importance of image by including the representation of the building on the labels - and the enormous bodegas of the Marco de Jerez. Today, the creation of new wineries combines the functionality of an industrial programme with technology, design and art. At a time when the passion for wine and its commercialisation is spreading around the world, producers are trying to consolidate their position in the market with an original and eloquent corporate image that illustrates the spirit of the winery. From the bottle and the label to the building itself, the design of each visual element is taken care of in detail, so that the new wineries and their production and marketing spaces are increasingly spaces of sociability, communication and the physical expression of a brand. The popularisation of wine culture has transformed wineries into leisure and tourism centres, to the extent that some include restaurants and hotels with oenotherapy treatments.

Indeed, winery architecture always appeals to a strong industrial and functional character, where space and volume are defined by the production process: the structure is often bought by the square metre, and the theme of the project concentrates on the definition of materials and the design of façades and roofs. Generally speaking, the association of two disciplines as demanding as architecture and winemaking aims to offer the best conditions for winemaking. The functionality of materials and space, the achievement of appropriate thermal conditions and integration into the natural environment are fundamental requirements. The projects in this compilation constitute an essential sample of the architectural possibilities offered by the design of any winery; in short, buildings that house and shape the complex world of wine.

Obwohl die Architektur im Zusammenhang mit der Welt des Weins in den letzten zehn Jahren einen regelrechten Boom erlebt hat, da es scheinbar keine große Weinkellerei gibt, die nicht ein interessantes Projekt hat, ist die Wahrheit, dass schon in den Ursprüngen der Weinbereitung große architektonische Werke durchgeführt wurden. Zum Beispiel haben Weindörfer par excellence, wie Aranda de Duero oder Langenlois (Österreich), kilometerlange unterirdische Gänge zur Lagerung ihrer kostbaren Weine, die bis ins Mittelalter zurückreichen. Später kamen die berühmten Erzeuger aus Bordeaux und ihre prächtigen Chateaux - die als erste die Bedeutung des Images erkannten, indem sie die Darstellung des Gebäudes auf die Etiketten aufnahmen - und die riesigen Bodegas des Marco de Jerez. Heute wird bei der Schaffung neuer Weingüter die Funktionalität eines industriellen Programms mit Technologie, Design und Kunst kombiniert. In einer Zeit, in der sich die Leidenschaft für Wein und seine Kommerzialisierung auf der ganzen Welt ausbreitet, versuchen die Produzenten, ihre Position auf dem Markt mit einem originellen und eloquenten Erscheinungsbild zu festigen, das den Geist der Kellerei veranschaulicht. Von der Flasche über das Etikett bis hin zum Gebäude selbst wird auf die Gestaltung jedes visuellen Elements geachtet, so dass die neuen Weinkellereien und ihre Produktions- und Marketingräume immer mehr zu Räumen der Geselligkeit, der Kommunikation und des physischen Ausdrucks einer Marke werden. Die Popularisierung der Weinkultur hat die Weingüter in Freizeit- und Tourismuszentren verwandelt, und zwar in einem Maße, dass einige Restaurants und Hotels mit Önotherapie-Behandlungen umfassen.

In der Tat spricht die Architektur von Weingütern immer einen starken industriellen und funktionalen Charakter an, bei dem Raum und Volumen durch den Produktionsprozess definiert werden: die Struktur wird oft nach Quadratmetern gekauft, und das Thema des Projekts konzentriert sich auf die Definition von Materialien und die Gestaltung von Fassaden und Dächern. Generell zielt die Verbindung von zwei so anspruchsvollen Disziplinen wie Architektur und Weinbau darauf ab, die besten Bedingungen für den Weinbau zu bieten. Die Funktionalität von Material und Raum, das Erreichen angemessener thermischer Bedingungen und die Integration in die natürliche Umgebung sind grundlegende Anforderungen. Die Projekte in dieser Zusammenstellung stellen ein wesentliches Beispiel für die architektonischen Möglichkeiten dar, die die Gestaltung eines Weinguts bietet; kurz gesagt, Gebäude, die die komplexe Welt des Weins beherbergen und gestalten.

Bien que l'architecture associée au monde du vin ait connu un véritable essor ces dix dernières années, puisqu'il semble qu'il n'y ait pas une seule grande cave qui n'ait pas un projet intéressant, la vérité est que même aux origines de l'élaboration du vin, de grandes œuvres architecturales ont été réalisées. Par exemple, les villages viticoles par excellence, comme Aranda de Duero ou Langenlois (Autriche), possèdent des kilomètres de galeries souterraines pour stocker leurs précieux vins, qui remontent au Moyen Âge. Plus tard sont venus les célèbres producteurs de Bordeaux et leurs magnifiques châteaux - qui ont été les premiers à reconnaître l'importance de l'image en incluant la représentation du bâtiment sur les étiquettes - et les énormes bodegas du Marco de Jerez. Aujourd'hui, la création de nouvelles caves combine la fonctionnalité d'un programme industriel avec la technologie, le design et l'art. À l'heure où la passion du vin et sa commercialisation se répandent dans le monde entier, les producteurs tentent de consolider leur position sur le marché avec une image corporative originale et éloquente qui illustre l'esprit de la cave. De la bouteille et de l'étiquette au bâtiment lui-même, la conception de chaque élément visuel est soignée dans les moindres détails, de sorte que les nouvelles caves et leurs espaces de production et de commercialisation sont de plus en plus des espaces de sociabilité, de communication et d'expression physique d'une marque. La popularisation de la culture du vin a transformé les domaines viticoles en centres de loisirs et de tourisme, à tel point que certains comprennent des restaurants et des hôtels avec des traitements d'œnothérapie.

En effet, l'architecture des caves fait toujours appel à un fort caractère industriel et fonctionnel, où l'espace et le volume sont définis par le processus de production : la structure est souvent achetée au mètre carré, et le thème du projet se concentre sur la définition des matériaux et la conception des façades et des toits. D'une manière générale, l'association de deux disciplines aussi exigeantes que l'architecture et la viticulture vise à offrir les meilleures conditions pour la vinification. La fonctionnalité des matériaux et de l'espace, l'obtention de conditions thermiques appropriées et l'intégration dans l'environnement naturel sont des exigences fondamentales. Les projets présentés dans cette compilation constituent un échantillon essentiel des possibilités architecturales offertes par la conception de tout établissement vinicole ; en bref, des bâtiments qui abritent et façonnent le monde complexe du vin.

A pesar de que la arquitectura asociada al mundo del vino ha experimentado un verdadero *boom* en los últimos diez años, pues parece que no hay bodega importante que no cuente con un proyecto interesante, lo cierto es que ya en los orígenes de la preparación del vino se realizaban grandes obras arquitectónicas. Por ejemplo, los pueblos vinateros por excelencia, como Aranda de Duero o Langenlois (Austria), cuentan con kilómetros de galerías subterráneas para guardar sus preciados caldos, que se remontan al medioevo. Más tarde vendrían los afamados productores de Burdeos y sus magníficos chateaux –que serían los primeros en reconocer la importancia de la imagen al incluir la representación del edificio en las etiquetas–, y las enormes bodegas del Marco de Jerez. Actualmente, la creación de nuevas bodegas conjuga la funcionalidad propia de un programa industrial con tecnología, diseño y arte. En un momento en el que la pasión por el vino y su comercialización se extienden por el mundo entero, los productores intentan afianzar su posición en el mercado con una imagen corporativa original y elocuente que ilustre el espíritu de la bodega. Desde la botella y la etiqueta hasta el edificio en sí, el diseño de cada elemento visual se cuida al detalle, de manera que las nuevas bodegas y sus espacios de producción y comercialización son cada vez más espacios de sociabilidad, de comunicación y la expresión física de una marca. La popularización de la cultura del vino ha transformado las bodegas en centros de ocio y turismo, hasta el extremo de que algunas incluyen restaurantes y hoteles con tratamientos de enoterapia.

Efectivamente, la arquitectura de bodegas siempre apela a un fuerte carácter industrial y funcional, donde el espacio y el volumen quedan definidos por el proceso productivo: con frecuencia la estructura se compra por metro cuadrado, y el tema del proyecto se concentra en la definición de materiales y en el diseño de fachadas y cubiertas. En términos generales, la asociación de dos disciplinas tan exigentes como la arquitectura y la vitivinicultura tiene como objetivo ofrecer las mejores condiciones para la elaboración del vino. La funcionalidad de los materiales y del espacio, la obtención de condiciones térmicas apropiadas y la integración en el entorno natural son requerimientos fundamentales. Los proyectos de esta compilación constituyen una muestra esencial de las posibilidades arquitectónicas que ofrece el diseño de toda bodega; en definitiva, edificios que albergan y dan forma al complejo mundo del vino.

SEVERIN PROEKT
CÔTE ROCHEUSE WINERY
PHOTO © DANIEL ANNENKOV

2B&G (BELLIA-BOMBARA-GIANNETTO INGEGNERI) + AMORE CAMPIONE ARCHITETTURA

WWW.STUDIOACA.COM

> CANTINA GRACI

2B&G is an engineering firm founded by ingg Bellia, Bombara and Giannetto in 1991, in Castiglione di Sicilia. 2B&G has great experience in the realization of several works in Taormina Etna/Alcantara area. Many works were developed in 30 years of activity, as new constructions and renovations: residentials, industrials, commercials, hotels, farmhouses, agricampings; agricultural processing plants and several wine cellars in the Etna area. ACA Amore Campione Architettura was found in 2010 by Sebastiano Amore and Angela Maria Campione, in Catania. The studio joins the architectural theory with the research of experimentation, receiving many international awards: finalist in Young Italian Architects, 3rd. in the NIB Award, recommended for the Quadranti di Architettura and winner of Bellini award. In 2019 the studio won the national Dedalo Minosse award in "under 40" category.

2B&G ist ein Ingenieurbüro, das 1991 von ingg Bellia, Bombara und Giannetto in Castiglione di Sicilia gegründet wurde. 2B&G hat eine große Erfahrung in der Realisierung von verschiedenen Arbeiten im Bereich Taormina Ätna/Alcantara. In den 30 Jahren ihrer Tätigkeit hat sie zahlreiche Werke entwickelt, sowohl Neubauten als auch Renovierungen: Wohn-, Industrie- und Geschäftsgebäude, Hotels, Landhäuser, Agro-Camps; landwirtschaftliche Verarbeitungsbetriebe und mehrere Weinkellereien im Ätna-Gebiet. ACA Amore Campione Architettura wurde 2010 von Sebastiano Amore und Angela Maria Campione, in Catania gegründet. Das Studio vereint architektonische Theorie mit experimenteller Forschung und erhielt zahlreiche internationale Auszeichnungen: Finalist bei Young Italian Architects, 3. beim NIB Award, empfohlen für den Quadranti di Architettura und Gewinner des Bellini Award. Im Jahr 2019 gewann das Studio den nationalen Dedalo Minosse Award in der Kategorie „unter 40".

2B&G + ACA

2B&G est une société d'ingénierie fondée par ingg Bellia, Bombara et Giannetto en 1991, à Castiglione di Sicilia. 2B&G a une grande expérience dans la réalisation de plusieurs travaux dans la zone de Taormina Etna/Alcantara. En 30 ans d'activité, elle a réalisé de nombreux ouvrages, qu'il s'agisse de nouvelles constructions ou de rénovations : résidentiels, industriels, commerciaux, hôtels, maisons de campagne, agro-camps ; usines de transformation agricole et plusieurs établissements vinicoles dans la région de l'Etna. ACA Amore Campione Architettura a été fondée en 2010 par Sebastiano Amore et Angela Maria Campione, à Catane. Le studio unit la théorie architecturale à la recherche expérimentale, recevant de nombreux prix internationaux : finaliste du concours Jeunes architectes italiens, 3e du prix NIB, recommandé pour le Quadranti di Architettura et lauréat du prix Bellini. En 2019, le studio a remporté le prix national Dedalo Minosse dans la catégorie « moins de 40 ans ».

2B&G es una empresa de ingeniería fundada por ingg Bellia, Bombara y Giannetto en 1991, en Castiglione di Sicilia. 2B&G tiene una gran experiencia en la realización de varias obras en la zona de Taormina Etna/Alcantara. En 30 años de actividad se han desarrollado numerosas obras, tanto de nueva construcción como de renovación: residenciales, industriales, comerciales, hoteles, casas de campo, agro campamentos; plantas de procesamiento agrícola y varias bodegas en la zona del Etna. ACA Amore Campione Architettura fue fundada en 2010 por Sebastiano Amore y Angela Maria Campione, en Catania. El estudio une la teoría arquitectónica con la investigación de la experimentación, recibiendo numerosos premios internacionales: finalista en Jóvenes Arquitectos Italianos, 3º en el Premio NIB, recomendado para los Quadranti di Architettura y ganador del premio Bellini. En 2019 el estudio ganó el premio nacional Dedalo Minosse en la categoría "under 40".

The winery is located in an agricultural area in Passopisciaro, in Castiglione di Sicilia, characterized by the typical Etna rural landscape and vineyards. The new building is an extension of the existing winery historically owned by Graci's family. It's hypogeum, solid and compact. The main façade is oriented towards the vineyard. It disappears into the ground without hitting the historical. Boulders of black lava rocks are located partially covering the entrance as material of excavation. The building is dissolved into the skyline without creating any contraposition with the historical winery. The idea is to create symmetry between the embankment and the open field facing south. The symmetry line is emphasized by the staircase and the water drainage. A recess excavated in the rock shows the stratigraphy of the terrain under the vineyard, representing also the tasting area.

La cave est située dans une zone agricole à Passopisciaro, à Castiglione di Sicilia, caractérisée par le paysage rural typique de l'Etna et des vignobles. Le nouveau bâtiment est une extension de la cave existante, historiquement détenue par la famille Graci. Elle est hypogée, solide et compacte. La façade principale fait face au vignoble. Il disparaît dans le sol sans se confondre avec l'historique. Des blocs de roches de lave noire recouvrent partiellement l'entrée comme matériel d'excavation. Le bâtiment se fond dans l'horizon sans créer de contraste avec le domaine viticole historique. L'idée est de créer une symétrie entre le talus et le champ ouvert orienté vers le sud. La ligne de symétrie est soulignée par l'escalier et l'évacuation des eaux. Une fente creusée dans la roche montre la stratigraphie du terrain sous le vignoble, représentant également la zone de dégustation.

Das Weingut befindet sich in einem landwirtschaftlichen Gebiet in Passopisciaro, in Castiglione di Sicilia, das durch die typische ländliche Landschaft des Ätna und der Weinberge gekennzeichnet ist. Das neue Gebäude ist eine Erweiterung des bestehenden Weinguts, das sich historisch gesehen im Besitz der Familie Graci befindet. Es ist hypogäisch, solide und kompakt. Die Hauptfassade ist dem Weinberg zugewandt. Es verschwindet im Boden, ohne mit dem Historischen zu kollidieren. Felsbrocken aus schwarzem Lavagestein bedecken als Aushubmaterial teilweise den Eingang. Das Gebäude löst sich im Horizont auf, ohne einen Kontrast zum historischen Weingut zu bilden. Die Idee ist, eine Symmetrie zwischen der Böschung und dem offenen Feld nach Süden zu schaffen. Die Symmetrielinie wird durch die Treppe und die Wasserableitung hervorgehoben. Ein in den Fels gegrabener Spalt zeigt die Stratigraphie des Geländes unter dem Weinberg, der auch den Verkostungsbereich darstellt.

La bodega se encuentra en una zona agrícola en Passopisciaro, en Castiglione di Sicilia, caracterizada por el típico paisaje rural del Etna y los viñedos. El nuevo edificio es una ampliación de la bodega existente, históricamente propiedad de la familia Graci. Es hipogeo, sólido y compacto. La fachada principal está orientada hacia el viñedo. Desaparece en el suelo sin chocar con lo histórico. Los cantos rodados de rocas de lava negra se encuentran cubriendo parcialmente la entrada como material de excavación. El edificio se disuelve en el horizonte sin crear ninguna contraposición con la bodega histórica. La idea es crear una simetría entre el terraplén y el campo abierto orientado al sur. La línea de simetría se enfatiza con la escalera y el drenaje de agua. Una hendidura excavada en la roca muestra la estratigrafía del terreno bajo el viñedo, representando también la zona de degustación.

Section

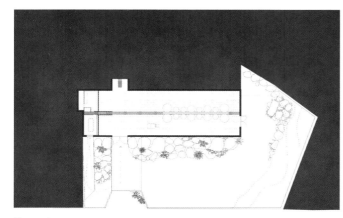

Floor plan

ALESSANDRO ISOLA STUDIO

WWW.ALESSANDROISOLA.COM

> LE MONDE WINERY. WINE TASTING ROOM /
OUTDOOR SPACE

LA FORZA
SCONVOLGENTE C
PENETRA L'UOMO
E NELLE
DISTRIB

Alessandro Isola studio is a multidisciplinary design practice based in London that specialises in architecture, interiors, and product design.

The studio was founded in 2014 by Alessandro Isola. Alessandro's formal training began at home in Italy, where he studied Art and Interior Architecture in Milan. He then headed to England and graduated in Architecture at the Oxford Brookes University School of Architecture, where he was granted a distinction and awarded the coveted Michael King memorial prize. He concluded his studies at the prestigious Architectural Association in London and worked for Foster + Partners where he also gained his RIBA/ARB professional chartered qualification. He co-founded IM Lab and subsequently started his practice in 2014.

With his creatively like-minded team, he works internationally with projects in England, United States, Switzerland, Russia and Italy. His projects and products have been exhibited, published, and awarded internationally.

Alessandro Isola Studio ist ein multidisziplinäres Designstudio mit Sitz in London, das sich auf Architektur, Inneneinrichtung und Produktdesign spezialisiert hat.

Das Studio wurde 2014 von Alessandro Isola gegründet. Alessandros Ausbildung begann in seinem Heimatland Italien, wo er in Mailand Kunst und Innenarchitektur studierte. Danach ging er nach England und machte seinen Abschluss in Architektur an der Oxford Brookes University School of Architecture, wo er eine Auszeichnung und den begehrten Michael King Memorial Award erhielt. Er schloss sein Studium an der renommierten Architectural Association in London ab und arbeitete für Foster + Partners, wo er auch seine RIBA/ARB Berufsqualifikation erwarb. Er ist Mitbegründer von IM Lab und hat 2014 sein Studio gegründet. Mit seinem Team von gleichgesinnten Kreativen arbeitet er international mit Projekten in England, USA, Schweiz, Russland und Italien. Seine Projekte und Produkte wurden international ausgestellt, veröffentlicht und ausgezeichnet.

ISOLA STUDIO

Il vino fulgido sul palato indugiava inghiottito.

Pigiare nel tino grappoli d'uva. Il calore del sole, ecco che cos'è.

E' come una carezza segreta che mi risveglia ricordi.

James Joyce

VINO

NE SPARGE E
CE L'ARDORE.

TITO LUCREZIO CARO

Grande è la fortuna
di colui che possiede
una buona bottiglia,
un buon libro,
un buon amico.

Molière

Vino pazzo che suo
e a ridere di gusto,
e lascia sfuggire qu

Alessandro Isola studio est un studio de design multidisciplinaire basé à Londres, spécialisé dans l'architecture, les intérieurs et le design de produits.

Le studio a été fondé en 2014 par Alessandro Isola. L'éducation d'Alessandro a commencé dans son pays natal, l'Italie, où il a étudié l'art et l'architecture d'intérieur à Milan. Il s'est ensuite rendu en Angleterre et a obtenu un diplôme d'architecture à l'école d'architecture de l'université Brookes d'Oxford, où il a obtenu une distinction et le très convoité Michael King memorial award. Il a terminé ses études à la prestigieuse Architectural Association de Londres et a travaillé pour Foster + Partners, où il a également obtenu sa qualification professionnelle RIBA/ARB. Il a cofondé IM Lab et a ensuite lancé son studio en 2014.

Avec son équipe d'esprits créatifs partageant les mêmes idées, il travaille au niveau international avec des projets en Angleterre, aux États-Unis, en Suisse, en Russie et en Italie. Ses projets et produits ont été exposés, publiés et récompensés au niveau international.

Alessandro Isola studio es un estudio de diseño multidisciplinar con sede en Londres especializado en arquitectura, interiores y diseño de productos.

El estudio fue fundado en 2014 por Alessandro Isola. La formación de Alessandro comenzó en su país, Italia, donde estudió Arte y Arquitectura de Interiores en Milán. A continuación, se dirigió a Inglaterra y se graduó en Arquitectura en la Escuela de Arquitectura de la Universidad de Oxford Brookes, donde obtuvo una distinción y el codiciado premio Michael King memorial. Concluyó sus estudios en la prestigiosa Architectural Association de Londres y trabajó para Foster + Partners, donde también obtuvo su título profesional RIBA/ARB. Fue cofundador de IM Lab y posteriormente puso en marcha su estudio en 2014.

Con su equipo de ideas afines a la creatividad, trabaja a nivel internacional con proyectos en Inglaterra, Estados Unidos, Suiza, Rusia e Italia. Sus proyectos y productos han sido expuestos, publicados y premiados internacionalmente.

The focus of the wine tasting room project was to create a space devoted to sensory experience that ensured a constant visual connection with the surrounding vineyard via the existing gallery windows. The overall result is a room that's at one with its surroundings and offers visitors a beautifully considered environment from which they can sample the award winning produce of this fine Italian winery. The outdoor space, part of the award-wining Le Monde Winery, is an architectural promenade offering the visitor an experiential journey of the surrounding Italian vineyards. The site houses both the winery and visitors centre, along with a guesthouse.

L'objectif du projet de salle de dégustation de vin était de créer un espace dédié à l'expérience sensorielle qui assurerait une connexion visuelle constante avec le vignoble environnant à travers les fenêtres de la galerie existante. Le résultat est une salle qui s'intègre dans son environnement et offre aux visiteurs un environnement bien aménagé pour déguster les produits primés de la cave italienne. L'espace extérieur, qui fait partie du domaine viticole primé Le Monde, est une promenade architecturale qui offre aux visiteurs un voyage expérientiel à travers les vignobles italiens environnants. Le site abrite à la fois la cave et le centre d'accueil, ainsi qu'une maison d'hôtes.

Das Ziel des Projekts für den Weinverkostungsraum war es, einen Raum zu schaffen, der dem sensorischen Erlebnis gewidmet ist und durch die vorhandenen Galeriefenster eine ständige visuelle Verbindung mit dem umliegenden Weinberg gewährleistet. Das Ergebnis ist ein Raum, der sich in seine Umgebung einfügt und den Besuchern eine gut ausgestattete Umgebung bietet, in der sie die preisgekrönten Produkte des italienischen Weinguts verkosten können. Der Außenbereich, Teil des preisgekrönten Weinguts Le Monde, ist eine architektonische Promenade, die Besuchern eine Erlebnisreise durch die umliegenden italienischen Weinberge bietet. Das Gelände beherbergt sowohl das Weingut und das Besucherzentrum als auch ein Gästehaus.

El objetivo del proyecto de la sala de cata de vinos era crear un espacio dedicado a la experiencia sensorial que garantizara una conexión visual constante con el viñedo circundante a través de las ventanas de la galería existente. El resultado es una sala que se integra en su entorno y ofrece a los visitantes un ambiente muy cuidado en el que pueden degustar los premiados productos de esta bodega italiana. El espacio exterior, que forma parte de la galardonada bodega Le Monde, es un paseo arquitectónico que ofrece al visitante un viaje experiencial por los viñedos italianos de los alrededores. El lugar alberga tanto la bodega como el centro de visitantes, además de una casa de huéspedes.

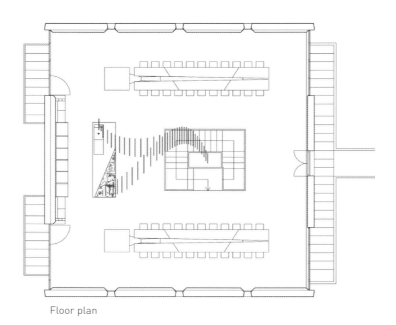

Floor plan

ALLIED

ALLIED WORKS

WWW.ALLIEDWORKS.COM

> SOKOL BLOSSER WINERY PAVILION

Allied Works is a collective of architects and creators who share a passion for design, and equally, the advancement of our social and environmental wellbeing. We are united by an ethic of boundless curiosity and uncommon commitment to creating beautiful, moving, and meaningful work.

Brad Cloepfil founded Allied Works in 1994 in Portland, Oregon. Since 2000, the practice has grown steadily through the completion of major arts and cultural projects, innovative educational facilities, residences and workplaces of diverse scale, purpose, and character.

Recently completed projects include Davies and Brook, the new restaurant at Claridge's, London; the expansion of Providence Park Stadium in Portland, Oregon; the National Veterans Memorial and Museum in Columbus, Ohio; *Uniqlo City*, the global headquarters and creative studios for Fast Retailing in Tokyo, Japan; the National Music Centre of Canada in Calgary, Alberta; and the Clyfford Still Museum in Denver, Colorado.

Allied Works ist ein Kollektiv von Architekten und Kreativen, die die Leidenschaft für Design und gleichzeitig die Förderung unseres sozialen und ökologischen Wohlbefindens teilen. Uns verbindet eine Ethik der grenzenlosen Neugier und ein ungewöhnliches Engagement, schöne, bewegende und bedeutungsvolle Arbeiten zu schaffen.

Brad Cloepfil gründete Allied Works im Jahr 1994 in Portland, Oregon. Seit dem Jahr 2000 ist das Studio durch die Realisierung großer Kunst- und Kulturprojekte, innovativer Bildungsinstallationen, Residenzen und Arbeitsplätze unterschiedlichen Umfangs, Zwecks und Charakters stetig gewachsen.

Zu den jüngsten Projekten gehören Davies and Brook, das neue Restaurant im Claridge's in London; die Erweiterung des Providence Park Stadions in Portland, Oregon; das National Veterans Memorial and Museum in Columbus, Ohio; Uniqlo City, der weltweite Hauptsitz und die Kreativstudios von Fast Retailing in Tokio, Japan; das Canadian National Music Centre in Calgary, Alberta; und das Clyfford Still Museum in Denver, Colorado.

WORKS

© Skyris Imaging

Allied Works est un collectif d'architectes et de créateurs qui partagent une passion pour le design et, parallèlement, pour l'avancement de notre bien-être social et environnemental. Nous sommes unis par une éthique de curiosité illimitée et un engagement hors du commun à créer des œuvres belles, émouvantes et significatives.

Brad Cloepfil a fondé Allied Works en 1994 à Portland, dans l'Oregon. Depuis 2000, le studio n'a cessé de se développer grâce à la réalisation de grands projets artistiques et culturels, d'installations éducatives innovantes, de résidences et de lieux de travail d'envergure, d'objectif et de caractère différents.

Parmi les projets récents, citons Davies and Brook, le nouveau restaurant du Claridge's à Londres ; l'agrandissement du stade Providence Park à Portland, dans l'Oregon ; le National Veterans Memorial and Museum à Columbus, dans l'Ohio ; Uniqlo City, le siège mondial et les studios de création de Fast Retailing à Tokyo, au Japon ; le Centre national de la musique canadienne à Calgary, dans l'Alberta ; et le Clyfford Still Museum à Denver, dans le Colorado.

Allied Works es un colectivo de arquitectos y creadores que comparten la pasión por el diseño y, al mismo tiempo, el avance de nuestro bienestar social y medioambiental. Nos une una ética de curiosidad ilimitada y un compromiso poco común con la creación de obras bellas, conmovedoras y significativas.

Brad Cloepfil fundó Allied Works en 1994 en Portland, Oregón. Desde el año 2000, el estudio ha crecido de forma constante gracias a la realización de importantes proyectos artísticos y culturales, innovadoras instalaciones educativas, residencias y lugares de trabajo de diversa escala, propósito y carácter.

Entre los proyectos más recientes figuran Davies and Brook, el nuevo restaurante del Claridge's de Londres; la ampliación del estadio Providence Park de Portland (Oregón); el Museo y Monumento Nacional a los Veteranos de Columbus (Ohio); Uniqlo City, la sede mundial y los estudios creativos de Fast Retailing en Tokio (Japón); el Centro Nacional de Música de Canadá en Calgary (Alberta); y el Museo Clyfford Still de Denver (Colorado).

The design of the Tasting Room begins with the land. A series of terraces are stepped into the rolling contours of the surrounding Dundee Hills, a region that produces some of the finest Pinot Noirs in the world. Bordered by meandering site walls and native vegetation, these terraces form gardens, outdoor event spaces, and parking courts that are woven into the landscape. Occupying the center terrace, the Tasting Room spans gracefully between the existing winery and a mature grove of oak trees. Covered with a living roof and held close to the ground, the building reads as an extruded mass of earth carved by light to form new gathering places and passages through the site. Inside and out, the building is clad in striated cedar that presents a warm and organic architectural form derived from the patterning of vineyard rows and vernacular wood agricultural buildings of the region.

La conception de la salle de dégustation commence par le terrain lui-même. Une série de terrasses s'avance dans les contours ondulés des collines de Dundee, une région qui produit certains des meilleurs pinots noirs du monde. Bordées de murs sinueux et de végétation indigène, ces terrasses forment des jardins, des espaces événementiels extérieurs et des cours de stationnement qui s'entremêlent avec le paysage. La salle de dégustation, qui occupe la terrasse centrale, s'étend élégamment entre la cave existante et un bosquet de chênes. Recouvert d'un toit vivant et accroché au sol à une extrémité, le bâtiment se présente comme une masse extrudée de terre sculptée par la lumière pour former de nouveaux lieux de rassemblement et des passages. À l'intérieur comme à l'extérieur, le bâtiment est revêtu de cèdre cannelé qui présente une forme architecturale organique et chaleureuse inspirée des rangées de vignes et des bâtiments agricoles en bois de la région.

Die Gestaltung des Verkostungsraums beginnt mit dem Gelände selbst. Eine Reihe von Terrassen ragt in die sanften Konturen der Hügel von Dundee, einer Region, die einige der besten Pinot Noirs der Welt hervorbringt. Eingefasst von mäandrierenden Mauern und einheimischer Vegetation bilden diese Terrassen Gärten, Veranstaltungsflächen im Freien und Parkhöfe, die sich in die Landschaft einfügen. Der Verkostungsraum, der die zentrale Terrasse einnimmt, erstreckt sich elegant zwischen dem bestehenden Keller und einem Hain aus Eichen. Mit einem lebendigen Dach bedeckt und an einem Ende an den Boden geklammert, liest sich das Gebäude wie eine extrudierte Masse aus Erde, die vom Licht geformt wurde, um neue Versammlungsorte und Passagen zu bilden. Sowohl innen als auch außen ist das Gebäude mit geriffeltem Zedernholz verkleidet, das eine warme, organische architektonische Form aufweist, die sich aus dem Muster der Weinbergreihen und den traditionellen hölzernen Farmgebäuden der Region ableitet.

El diseño de la sala de degustación comienza con el propio terreno. Una serie de terrazas se adentran en los contornos ondulados de las colinas de Dundee, una región que produce algunos de los mejores Pinot Noir del mundo. Bordeadas por muros serpenteantes y vegetación autóctona, estas terrazas forman jardines, espacios para eventos al aire libre y patios de aparcamiento que se entrelazan con el paisaje. La sala de degustación, que ocupa la terraza central, se extiende con elegancia entre la bodega existente y un bosquecillo de robles. Cubierto con un techo vivo y pegado al suelo en uno de sus extremos, el edificio se lee como una masa extruida de tierra tallada por la luz para formar nuevos lugares de reunión y pasajes. Tanto en el interior como en el exterior, el edificio está revestido de cedro estriado que presenta una forma arquitectónica cálida y orgánica derivada del patrón de las hileras de viñedos y de los edificios agrícolas de madera vernáculos de la región.

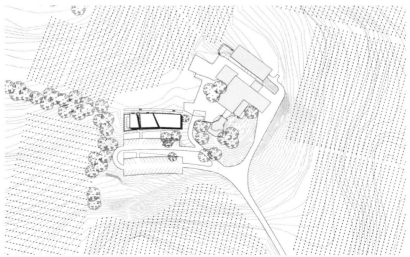

Site plan

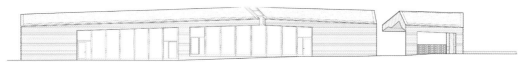

North elevation

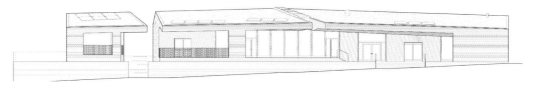

South elevation

ANDREAS BURGHARDT

WWW.BURGHARDT.CO.AT

> FRED LOIMER
> NEUMEISTER WEINGUT
> NIEPOORT WINERY

Andreas Burghardt lives in Vienna, Austria, since 1962. Established his own office there in 1995. Works include clients like EY, Oracle, IBM, Generali, Swatchgroup, Signa, Borealis and others, as well as historic buildings, small scale projects, and graphic design.

Has been involved in projects for the wine industry for Fred Loimer, Niepoort Vinhos, Dorli Muhr, Albert Neumeister.

Developed even the graphic design for the logos and labels of Fred Loimer, Albert Neumeister, Kappa Rosso, and Schellmann.

Andreas Burghardt lebt seit 1962 in Wien (Österreich). Dort gründete er 1995 sein eigenes Büro. Zu seinen Arbeiten gehören Kunden wie EY, Oracle, IBM, Generali, Swatchgroup, Signa, Borealis und andere, aber auch historische Gebäude, kleinere Projekte und Grafikdesignarbeiten.

Er hat Projekte für die Weinindustrie für Fred Loimer, Niepoort Vinhos, Dorli Muhr und Albert Neumeister durchgeführt.

Er entwickelte auch das grafische Design von Logos und Etiketten für Fred Loimer, Albert Neumeister, Kappa Rosso und Schellmann.

BURGHARDT

Andreas Burghardt vit à Vienne (Autriche) depuis 1962. Il y a établi son propre bureau en 1995. Il travaille pour des clients tels que EY, Oracle, IBM, Generali, Swatchgroup, Signa, Borealis et d'autres, ainsi que pour des bâtiments historiques, des projets à petite échelle et des travaux de conception graphique.

Il a réalisé des projets pour l'industrie du vin pour Fred Loimer, Niepoort Vinhos, Dorli Muhr et Albert Neumeister.

Il a également développé la conception graphique des logos et des étiquettes pour Fred Loimer, Albert Neumeister, Kappa Rosso et Schellmann.

Andreas Burghardt vive en Viena (Austria) desde 1962. Estableció allí su propia oficina en 1995. Sus trabajos incluyen clientes como EY, Oracle, IBM, Generali, Swatchgroup, Signa, Borealis y otros, así como edificios históricos, proyectos a pequeña escala y trabajos de diseño gráfico.

Ha realizado proyectos para la industria del vino para Fred Loimer, Niepoort Vinhos, Dorli Muhr y Albert Neumeister.

Desarrolló incluso el diseño gráfico de los logotipos y etiquetas de Fred Loimer, Albert Neumeister, Kappa Rosso y Schellmann.

Fred Loimer is one of the most prolific winemakers in Austria. The winery, built in 1998 is an icon of Austrian wine architecture, the first example of modern architecture in the wine scene and at that time a scandal in the rural area because of its radical black box design.
The tasting and office building is an atrium, hermetically closed to the exterior with only one single window framing the landscape with the Heiligenstein mountain, one of best of Loimer´s wineyards.
The reduced, not to say minimalistic architecture, represents Fred Loimer´s philosophy of purity and straightness. The project is a successful example how architecture supports the public image and message and has a big impact on a trademark. The architect even designed the logo and all labels up to now for the last 20 years.

Fred Loimer est l´un des vignerons les plus prolifiques d´Autriche. Sa cave, construite en 1998, est une icône de l´architecture viticole autrichienne, le premier exemple d´architecture moderne sur la scène viticole et, à l´époque, un scandale dans la campagne pour sa conception radicale de boîte noire.
Le bâtiment de dégustation et de bureaux est un atrium hermétiquement fermé, avec une seule fenêtre encadrant le paysage avec la montagne Heiligenstein, l´un des meilleurs vignobles de Loimer.
L´architecture réduite, pour ne pas dire minimaliste, représente la philosophie de pureté et de rectitude de Fred Loimer. Le projet est un exemple réussi de la manière dont l´architecture soutient l´image et le message publics et a un grand impact sur une marque. L´architecte a même conçu le logo et toutes les étiquettes depuis 20 ans.

Fred Loimer ist einer der produktivsten Winzer Österreichs. Sein 1998 erbautes Weingut ist eine Ikone der österreichischen Weinarchitektur, das erste Beispiel für moderne Architektur in der Weinszene und damals ein Skandal auf dem Lande wegen seines radikalen Black-Box-Designs.
Das Verkostungs- und Bürogebäude ist ein hermetisch abgeschlossenes Atrium mit einem einzigen Fenster, das die Landschaft mit dem Heiligenstein, einer der besten Weinlagen Loimers, einrahmt.
Die reduzierte, um nicht zu sagen minimalistische, Architektur repräsentiert Fred Loimers Philosophie der Reinheit und Geradlinigkeit. Das Projekt ist ein gelungenes Beispiel dafür, wie Architektur das öffentliche Image und die Botschaft unterstützt und eine große Wirkung auf eine Marke hat. Der Architekt hat sogar das Logo und alle Etiketten der letzten 20 Jahre entworfen.

Fred Loimer es uno de los viticultores más prolíficos de Austria. Su bodega, construida en 1998, es un icono de la arquitectura vitivinícola austriaca, el primer ejemplo de arquitectura moderna en el panorama del vino y, en su momento, un escándalo en la zona rural por su radical diseño de caja negra.
El edificio de catas y oficinas es un atrio herméticamente cerrado al exterior con una sola ventana que enmarca el paisaje con la montaña Heiligenstein, uno de los mejores viñedos de Loimer.
La arquitectura reducida, por no decir minimalista, representa la filosofía de pureza y rectitud de Fred Loimer. El proyecto es un exitoso ejemplo de cómo la arquitectura apoya la imagen y el mensaje públicos y tiene un gran impacto en una marca. El arquitecto incluso ha diseñado el logotipo y todas las etiquetas de los últimos 20 años.

NEUMEISTER WEINGUT
STRADEN, AUSTRIA

Albert Neumeister and his son Christoph are prolific white wine makers in Styria, well known for their sharply conceived and precise whitewines.

This project was challenging because the former architect who designed the building itself abandoned the project and his client. So what Andreas Burghardt was confronted with in the year 2000 was an unfinished building and a desperate client. The project consisted in the reconstruction of a new, unfinished building. The tasting area is completely below ground and built in exposed concrete.

10.000 bottles have precisely been placed as a huge sculpture. The wall of bottles was a simple but effective idea to improve acoustics and divdide the different areas. All other areas are covered in wood, using oiled elm to create a cosy athmosphere.

Albert Neumeister et son fils Christoph sont des producteurs prolifiques de vins blancs en Styrie, bien connus pour leurs vins blancs conçus avec précision.

Ce projet était un défi car le précédent architecte qui avait conçu le bâtiment a abandonné le projet et son client. En 2000, Andreas Burghardt a donc trouvé un bâtiment inachevé et un client désespéré. Le projet consistait en la reconstruction d'un bâtiment neuf et inachevé. L'espace de dégustation est entièrement souterrain et fait de béton apparent.

10 000 bouteilles ont été placées avec précision sous la forme d'une immense sculpture. Le mur de bouteilles était une idée simple mais efficace pour améliorer l'acoustique et diviser les différentes zones. Tous les autres espaces sont habillés de bois, avec de l'orme huilé pour créer une atmosphère chaleureuse.

Albert Neumeister und sein Sohn Christoph sind produktive Weißweinproduzenten in der Steiermark, bekannt für ihre präzise konzipierten Weißweine.

Dieses Projekt war eine Herausforderung, weil der vorherige Architekt, der das Gebäude entworfen hat, das Projekt und seinen Kunden im Stich gelassen hat. Was Andreas Burghardt also im Jahr 2000 vorfand, war ein unfertiges Gebäude und ein verzweifelter Bauherr. Das Projekt bestand aus dem Wiederaufbau eines neuen, noch nicht fertiggestellten Gebäudes. Der Verkostungsbereich ist komplett unterirdisch und besteht aus Sichtbeton.

10.000 Flaschen wurden präzise in Form einer riesigen Skulptur platziert. Die Flaschenwand war eine einfache, aber effektive Idee, um die Akustik zu verbessern und die verschiedenen Bereiche zu unterteilen. Alle anderen Bereiche sind mit Holz verkleidet, wobei geölte Ulme für eine gemütliche Atmosphäre sorgt.

Albert Neumeister y su hijo Christoph son prolíficos productores de vino blanco en Estiria, bien conocidos por sus vinos blancos de concepción precisa.

Este proyecto supuso un reto porque el anterior arquitecto que diseñó el edificio abandonó el proyecto y a su cliente. Así que lo que Andreas Burghardt se encontró en el año 2000 fue un edificio inacabado y un cliente desesperado. El proyecto consistía en la reconstrucción de un edificio nuevo e inacabado. La zona de degustación está completamente bajo tierra y construida en hormigón visto.

Se han colocado con precisión 10.000 botellas en forma de enorme escultura. El muro de botellas fue una idea sencilla pero eficaz para mejorar la acústica y dividir las distintas zonas. Todas las demás áreas están revestidas de madera, utilizando olmo aceitado para crear un ambiente acogedor.

The winery is situated at the Tedo River a romantic branch of the Douro river high above in Napoles, Portugal, with a breathtaking view over the landscape. Impressive in size, construction and functionality, the minimalist design of the 5,000 m² winery leaves a maximum impact. It is energy-efficient and sustainable, using local materials and powered by solar panels. The winemaking process is done in the most logical and energy-efficient of ways: using gravity insted of pumping the grapes. For the façade the same slate was used to merge the building with the surrounding. The material concept is very reduced: the building consists of three main materials: stone, concrete and inox for the machinery. As the soil consists mostly of solid rock it was not possible to build an underground winery. The building was conceived as a terraced sculpture, continuing the existing ones.

La cave est située sur la rivière Tedo, un bras romantique de la rivière Douro, au-dessus de Naples (Portugal), avec une vue extraordinaire sur le paysage. Impressionnante par sa taille, sa construction et sa fonctionnalité, la conception minimaliste de la cave de 5.000 m² a un impact sur le visiteur. Il est économe en énergie et durable, utilisant des matériaux locaux et alimenté par des panneaux solaires. Le processus de vinification est réalisé de la manière la plus logique et la plus économe en énergie : en utilisant la gravité au lieu de pomper les raisins. La même ardoise a été utilisée pour la façade, ce qui permet au bâtiment de s'intégrer dans son environnement. Le concept des matériaux est très dépouillé : le bâtiment se compose de trois matériaux principaux : la pierre, le béton et l'acier inoxydable pour les machines. Le sol étant principalement constitué de roche solide, il n'était pas possible de construire une cave souterraine. Le bâtiment a été conçu comme une sculpture en terrasses, dans la continuité de celles existantes.

Das Weingut liegt am Tedo-Fluss, einem romantischen Seitenarm des Douro-Flusses, hoch über Neapel (Portugal), mit außergewöhnlichem Blick über die Landschaft. Beeindruckend in Größe, Konstruktion und Funktionalität wirkt das minimalistische Design des 5.000 m² großen Weinguts auf den Besucher. Es ist energieeffizient und nachhaltig, verwendet lokale Materialien und wird durch Solarzellen betrieben. Die Weinherstellung erfolgt auf die logischste und energieeffizienteste Art und Weise: mit Hilfe der Schwerkraft, anstatt die Trauben zu pumpen. Für die Fassade wurde der gleiche Schiefer verwendet, wodurch sich das Gebäude in die Umgebung einfügt. Das Materialkonzept ist sehr schlank: Das Gebäude besteht aus drei Hauptmaterialien: Stein, Beton und Edelstahl für die Maschinen. Da der Boden größtenteils aus festem Gestein besteht, war es nicht möglich, einen unterirdischen Keller zu bauen. Das Gebäude wurde als eine Skulptur in Terrassen konzipiert, die die bestehenden fortsetzt.

La bodega está situada en el río Tedo, un romántico brazo del río Duero, en lo alto de Nápoles (Portugal), con unas vistas extraordinarias. Impresionante por su tamaño, construcción y funcionalidad, el diseño minimalista de la bodega de 5.000 m² impacta al visitante. Es energéticamente eficiente y sostenible, utilizando materiales locales y alimentada por paneles solares. El proceso de elaboración del vino se realiza de la forma más lógica y eficiente desde el punto de vista energético: utilizando la gravedad en lugar de bombear la uva. Para la fachada se utilizó la misma pizarra, lo que permite fusionar el edificio con el entorno. El concepto de materiales es muy reducido: el edificio consta de tres materiales principales: piedra, hormigón e inox para la maquinaria. Como el suelo está formado en su mayor parte por roca sólida, no era posible construir una bodega subterránea. El edificio se concibió como una escultura en terrazas, continuando las ya existentes.

ARCHINGEGNO

WWW.ARCHINGEGNO.INFO

> CANTINA VALETTI

Since 1998 Archingegno has designed and built public, residential and tertiary buildings, with particular experience in the design of work spaces. The founding partners Carlo Ferrari and Alberto Pontiroli consider architecture an intertwining of historical and contemporary elements capable of producing something very special, giving personalized solutions that are unconventional and adaptable to different contexts. Users are inspired to feel a sense of belonging to their buildings. Archingegno seek to maintain cultural research alive, integrating into their projects the most advanced technologies and artisan skills, as well as the ever present vision of Italian design. Every single aspect, from choice of materials to physical and cultural contexts is taken into consideration in order to create a quintessential space.

Archingegno entwirft und baut seit 1998 öffentliche Gebäude, Wohngebäude und Gebäude des tertiären Sektors, mit besonderer Expertise in der Gestaltung von Arbeitsräumen. Die Gründungspartner Carlo Ferrari und Alberto Pontiroli betrachten Architektur als eine Verflechtung historischer und zeitgenössischer Elemente, die etwas ganz Besonderes hervorbringen kann und unkonventionelle, maßgeschneiderte Lösungen bietet, die sich an unterschiedliche Kontexte anpassen. Die Benutzer werden durch das Gefühl der Zugehörigkeit zu ihren Gebäuden inspiriert. Archingegno versucht, die kulturelle Forschung lebendig zu halten, indem es in seine Projekte die fortschrittlichsten Technologien und handwerklichen Fähigkeiten sowie die allgegenwärtige Vision des italienischen Designs integriert. Jeder Aspekt, von der Wahl der Materialien bis hin zu den physischen und kulturellen Kontexten, wird berücksichtigt, um einen Raum par excellence zu schaffen.

ARCHINGEGNO

Archingegno conçoit et réalise des bâtiments publics, résidentiels et tertiaires depuis 1998, avec une expertise particulière dans la conception d'espaces de travail. Les associés fondateurs Carlo Ferrari et Alberto Pontiroli considèrent que l'architecture est une imbrication d'éléments historiques et contemporains capable de produire quelque chose de très spécial, en fournissant des solutions personnalisées non conventionnelles adaptables à différents contextes. Les utilisateurs sont inspirés par le sentiment d'appartenance à leurs bâtiments. Archingegno s'efforce de maintenir vivante la recherche culturelle, en intégrant dans ses projets les technologies et les compétences artisanales les plus avancées, ainsi que la vision toujours présente du design italien. Chaque aspect, du choix des matériaux aux contextes physique et culturel, est pris en compte pour créer un espace par excellence.

Desde 1998 Archingegno diseña y construye edificios públicos, residenciales y terciarios, con especial experiencia en el diseño de espacios de trabajo. Los socios fundadores Carlo Ferrari y Alberto Pontiroli consideran que la arquitectura es un entrelazamiento de elementos históricos y contemporáneos capaz de producir algo muy especial, dando soluciones personalizadas poco convencionales y adaptables a diferentes contextos. Los usuarios se sienten inspirados por el sentido de pertenencia a sus edificios. Archingegno trata de mantener viva la investigación cultural, integrando en sus proyectos las tecnologías más avanzadas y las habilidades artesanales, así como la visión siempre presente del diseño italiano. Cada aspecto, desde la elección de los materiales hasta los contextos físicos y culturales, se tiene en cuenta para crear un espacio por excelencia.

Situated in the heart of Bardolino's Classical Production Area, Cantina Valetti, it has been obtaining the best from grapes by combining tradition with technology for three generations. The new wine cellar is composed of two above-ground levels for wine tasting, bottling and sales areas and an underground level for the production. The volume, a massive stone structure combined with a light steel structure, is a clear reference to the shapes and colours present in the typical elements of the surrounding landscape: the terraced stone walls and the stakes used to support the vines. The steel structure is made lighter thanks to the angles given to the outer supports which follow an "organic" reason; the stone wall is tilted towards the entrance's double height accompanying the visitor to the upper floors where a marvelous lake view opens up. At night, the building becomes iconic; the luminous lines, like graphic signs, reveal perspectives, views and volumes.

Située au cœur de la zone de production classique de Bardolino, la Cantina Valetti tire le meilleur du raisin depuis trois générations en alliant tradition et technologie. La nouvelle cave est composée de deux niveaux en surface pour les espaces de dégustation, de mise en bouteille et de vente, et d'un niveau souterrain pour la production. Le volume, une structure solide en pierre combinée à une structure légère en acier, est une référence claire aux formes et aux couleurs présentes dans les éléments typiques du paysage environnant : les murs de pierre en terrasse et les piquets utilisés pour soutenir les vignes. La structure en acier est allégée grâce aux angles donnés aux supports extérieurs qui suivent une logique « organique » ; le mur de pierre s'incline vers la double hauteur de l'entrée accompagnant le visiteur vers les étages supérieurs où s'ouvre une vue magnifique sur le lac. La nuit, le bâtiment devient iconique ; les lignes lumineuses, comme des signes graphiques, révèlent des perspectives, des vues et des volumes.

Im Herzen des klassischen Anbaugebiets von Bardolino gelegen, holt die Cantina Valetti seit drei Generationen das Beste aus den Trauben heraus, indem sie Tradition mit Technologie verbindet. Das neue Weingut besteht aus zwei oberirdischen Ebenen für Weinverkostung, Abfüllung und Verkaufsbereich und einer unterirdischen Ebene für die Produktion. Das Volumen, eine massive Steinkonstruktion in Kombination mit einer leichten Stahlkonstruktion, ist ein klarer Verweis auf die Formen und Farben, die in den typischen Elementen der umliegenden Landschaft zu finden sind: die terrassenförmigen Steinmauern und die Pfähle, die zur Unterstützung der Reben verwendet werden. Die Stahlkonstruktion ist dank der Winkel, die den äußeren Stützen gegeben wurden und die einem „organischen" Grund folgen, leichter; die Steinmauer neigt sich zur doppelten Höhe des Eingangs und begleitet den Besucher in die oberen Etagen, wo sich ein wunderbarer Blick auf den See eröffnet. Nachts wird das Gebäude ikonisch; die leuchtenden Linien, wie grafische Zeichen, offenbaren Perspektiven, Ansichten und Volumen.

Situada en el corazón de la zona de producción clásica de Bardolino, Cantina Valetti lleva tres generaciones obteniendo lo mejor de las uvas combinando tradición y tecnología. Se compone de dos niveles sobre el suelo para la degustación de vinos, el embotellado y las áreas de venta y un nivel subterráneo para la producción. El volumen, una estructura de piedra maciza combinada con una estructura ligera de acero, es una referencia a las formas y colores presentes en los elementos típicos del paisaje: los muros de piedra en terrazas y las estacas utilizadas para sostener las vides. La estructura de acero se aligera gracias a los ángulos dados a los soportes exteriores que siguen una razón "orgánica"; el muro de piedra se inclina hacia la doble altura de la entrada acompañando al visitante a las plantas superiores donde se abre una vista del lago. Por la noche, las líneas luminosas revelan perspectivas, vistas y volúmenes.

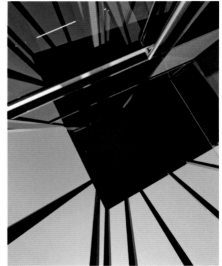

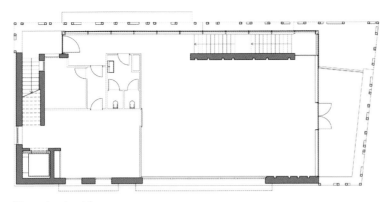

Floor plan level 1

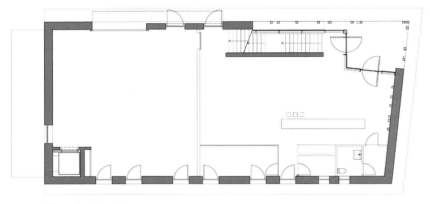

Floor plan level 0

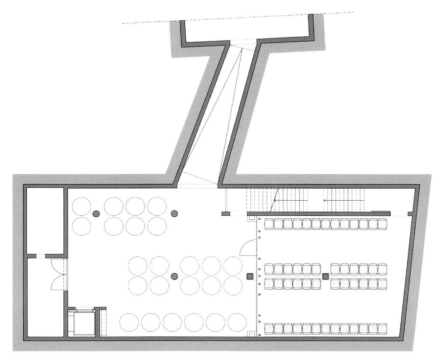

Floor plan level -1

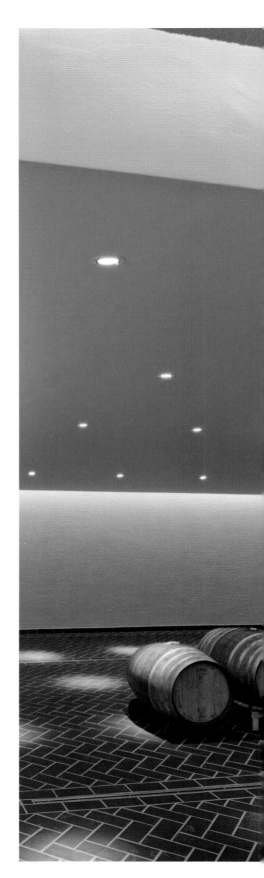

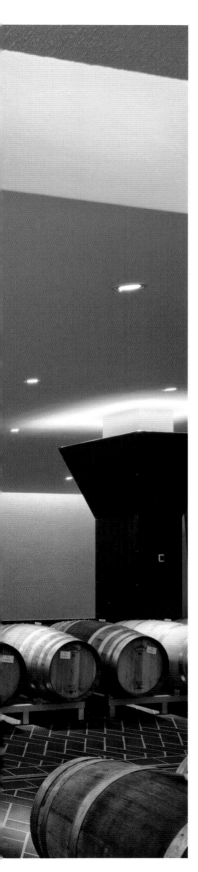

ARDESHIR NOZARI + ROSHAN NOZARI ARCHITECTS

WWW.NOZARIARCHITECTS.COM

> DARIOUSH WINERY

NOZARI +

The Los Angeles firm of Ardeshir Nozari + Roshan Nozari Architects, AIA, NCARB is known for designing unique residential, hospitality, and commercial projects. Each project is a creative collaboration between the architects and clients, greatly exemplified in Darioush Winery, an internationally acclaimed project, where the architects worked closely with the founders, Darioush and Shahpar Khaledi.

Ardeshir Nozari received the degree of Bachelor of Architecture from Tehran University and a Master of Architecture from the University of Southern California.

Roshan Ghaffarian Nozari received the degree of Bachelor of Science in Design and Environmental Analysis from Cornell University and a Master of Architecture from the University of California, Los Angeles.

Both principals are members of the American Institute of Architects and are certified by the National Council of Architectural Registration Board.

Das Studio von Ardeshir Nozari + Roshan Nozari Architects, AIA, NCARB in Los Angeles ist bekannt für die Gestaltung einzigartiger Wohn-, Gaststätten- und Gewerbeprojekte. Jedes Projekt ist eine kreative Zusammenarbeit zwischen den Architekten und den Bauherren. Das beste Beispiel dafür ist die Darioush Winery, ein international anerkanntes Projekt, bei dem die Architekten eng mit den Gründern, Darioush und Shahpar Khaledi, zusammenarbeiteten.

Ardeshir Nozari erhielt einen Bachelor-Abschluss in Architektur von der Universität Teheran und einen Master-Abschluss in Architektur von der University of Southern California.

Roshan Ghaffarian Nozari erwarb einen B.A. in Umweltdesign und -analyse an der Cornell University und einen M.A. in Architektur an der University of California, Los Angeles.

Beide Bauherren sind Mitglieder des American Institute of Architects und sind vom National Board of Registration of Architects zertifiziert.

NOZARI ARCHITECTS

© Chris Straughn

Le studio de Los Angeles d'Ardeshir Nozari + Roshan Nozari Architects, AIA, NCARB est connu pour la conception de projets résidentiels, commerciaux et d'accueil uniques. Chaque projet est le fruit d'une collaboration créative entre les architectes et les clients, comme en témoigne le projet Darioush Winery, un projet de renommée internationale, dans lequel les architectes ont travaillé en étroite collaboration avec les fondateurs, Darioush et Shahpar Khaledi.

Ardeshir Nozari a obtenu une licence d'architecture à l'université de Téhéran et une maîtrise d'architecture à l'université de Californie du Sud.

Roshan Ghaffarian Nozari est titulaire d'une licence en conception et analyse environnementales de l'université Cornell et d'une maîtrise en architecture de l'université de Californie, Los Angeles. Les deux directeurs sont membres de l'American Institute of Architects et sont certifiés par le National Board of Registration Board of Architects.

El estudio de Los Ángeles de Ardeshir Nozari + Roshan Nozari Architects, AIA, NCARB es conocido por diseñar proyectos residenciales, hosteleros y comerciales únicos. Cada proyecto es una colaboración creativa entre los arquitectos y los clientes, muy ejemplificada en Darioush Winery, un proyecto aclamado internacionalmente, en el que los arquitectos trabajaron estrechamente con los fundadores, Darioush y Shahpar Khaledi.

Ardeshir Nozari se licenció en arquitectura en la Universidad de Teherán y obtuvo un máster en arquitectura en la Universidad del Sur de California.

Roshan Ghaffarian Nozari se licenció en Diseño y Análisis Medioambiental por la Universidad de Cornell y obtuvo un máster en Arquitectura por la Universidad de California en Los Ángeles.

Ambos directores son miembros del Instituto Americano de Arquitectos y están certificados por el Consejo Nacional de la Junta de Registro de Arquitectos.

Darioush Winery, masterfully brings together the intricacy of historical elements with the minimalism of modern architecture and consistently attracts visitors nationally and internationally. A series of yellow travertine cladded pavilions, connected with glass and steel volumes, house the 2,300 m² structure. Various interpretations of the lotus flower, historically used to symbolize prosperity and affluence, are used to shape sixteen original casts, creating concrete moldings for the base, header, fascia and cornice. Sixteen entry stone columns, with two headed bull capitals, are reminiscent of the 21 m tall columns used in the Apadana Palace in Persepolis. They symbolize the trees of the garden of heaven, and mark the arrival at Darioush winery, setting the expectation for the memorable journey for the guests of experiencing the exquisite wine and spectacular architecture.

Le Darioush Winery associe de manière magistrale la complexité des éléments historiques au minimalisme de l'architecture moderne et attire régulièrement des visiteurs nationaux et internationaux. Une série de pavillons revêtus de travertin jaune, reliés par des volumes de verre et d'acier, abrite la structure de 2.300 m². Diverses interprétations de la fleur de lotus, historiquement utilisée pour symboliser la prospérité et la richesse, sont utilisées pour façonner seize moules originaux, créant ainsi des moulures en béton pour la base, la tête, le fascia et la corniche. Les seize colonnes de pierre de l'entrée, dont les chapiteaux sont constitués de deux têtes de taureau, rappellent les colonnes de 21 mètres de haut utilisées dans le palais d'Apadana à Persépolis. Ils symbolisent les arbres du jardin du paradis et marquent l'arrivée au domaine viticole de Darioush, laissant présager un voyage mémorable pour les invités qui découvriront un vin exquis et une architecture spectaculaire.

Darioush Winery vereint meisterhaft die Komplexität historischer Elemente mit dem Minimalismus moderner Architektur und zieht immer wieder nationale und internationale Besucher an. Eine Reihe von gelben, mit Travertin verkleideten Pavillons, die durch Volumen aus Glas und Stahl verbunden sind, beherbergen die 2.300 m² große Struktur. Verschiedene Interpretationen der Lotusblume, die historisch als Symbol für Wohlstand und Reichtum verwendet wird, werden verwendet, um sechzehn Originalformen zu formen, wobei Betonformteile für den Sockel, den Kopf, das Gesims und den Sims entstehen. Die sechzehn Steinsäulen am Eingang, mit Kapitellen aus zwei Stierköpfen, erinnern an die 21 Meter hohen Säulen des Apadana-Palastes in Persepolis. Sie symbolisieren die Bäume im Garten des Himmels und markieren die Ankunft in der Darioush Winery. Sie setzen die Erwartung einer unvergesslichen Reise für die Gäste, um den exquisiten Wein und die spektakuläre Architektur zu erleben.

La Bodega Darioush reúne magistralmente la complejidad de los elementos históricos con el minimalismo de la arquitectura moderna y atrae constantemente a visitantes nacionales e internacionales. Una serie de pabellones revestidos de travertino amarillo, conectados con volúmenes de vidrio y acero, albergan la estructura de 2.300 m². Varias interpretaciones de la flor de loto, utilizada históricamente para simbolizar la prosperidad y la riqueza, se utilizan para dar forma a dieciséis moldes originales, creando molduras de hormigón para la base, la cabecera, la imposta y la cornisa. Las dieciséis columnas de piedra de la entrada, con capiteles de dos cabezas de toro, recuerdan a las columnas de 21m de altura utilizadas en el palacio Apadana de Persépolis. Simbolizan los árboles del jardín del cielo y marcan la llegada a la bodega Darioush, estableciendo la expectativa de un viaje memorable de los huéspedes para experimentar el exquisito vino y la espectacular arquitectura.

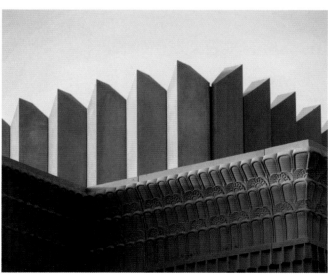

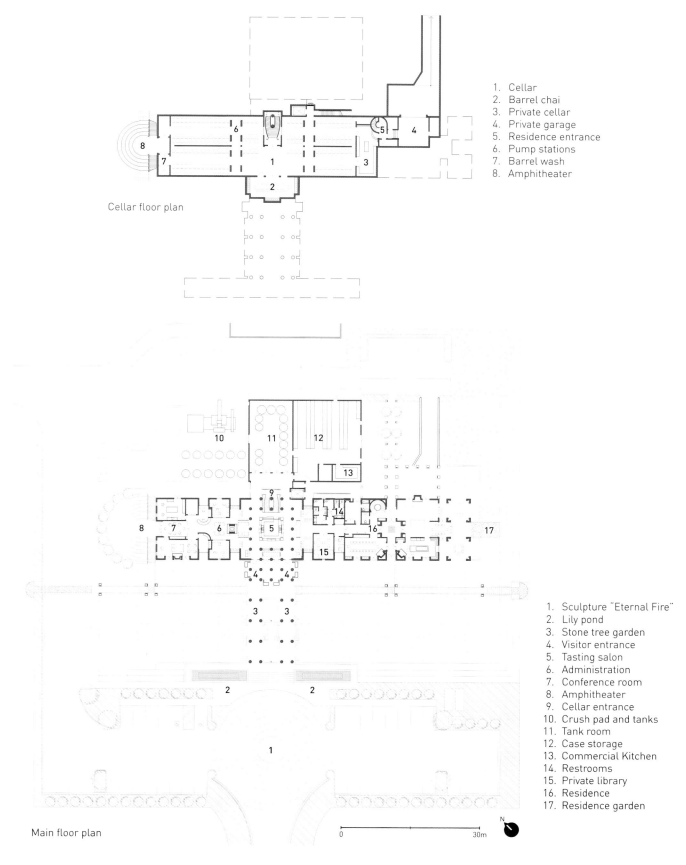

Cellar floor plan

1. Cellar
2. Barrel chai
3. Private cellar
4. Private garage
5. Residence entrance
6. Pump stations
7. Barrel wash
8. Amphitheater

Main floor plan

1. Sculpture "Eternal Fire"
2. Lily pond
3. Stone tree garden
4. Visitor entrance
5. Tasting salon
6. Administration
7. Conference room
8. Amphitheater
9. Cellar entrance
10. Crush pad and tanks
11. Tank room
12. Case storage
13. Commercial Kitchen
14. Restrooms
15. Private library
16. Residence
17. Residence garden

0   30m

N

BC ESTUDIO ARCHITECTS
JAVIER BARBA

WWW.BCESTUDIOARCHITECTS.COM

> WAULTRAUD CELLAR FOR BODEGAS TORRES
> WINERIE AND VISITOR CENTER.
  STAG'S LEAP WINE CELLAR WINERY
> STAG'S LEAP WINE CELLARS

BC Estudio Architects, founded by Javier Barba, is a solid team of professionals of different nationalities who share a vision and a method of design that have characterized the firm from its origins, with excellent results, as demonstrated in projects around the world. We are an architectural firm located in Barcelona with 40 years of international experience in the world of architecture design and pioneers in Green Architecture. Cultural, social, landscape and environmental values of the land are integrated into our architecture in order to guarantee the successful interpretation of our clients expectations and requirements. We understand architecture design as a tool to change and improve society. Our projects are designed with an overall, integrated architectural vision, blending the architecture, interior design and landscape design disciplines. Our architectural design creates an impact due to its beauty and functionality, so that function and emotion exist in harmony.

BC Estudio Arquitectos, gegründet von Javier Barba, ist ein solides Team von Fachleuten verschiedener Nationalitäten, die eine Vision und eine Design-Methode teilen, die das Büro seit seinen Anfängen charakterisieren, mit hervorragenden Ergebnissen, wie in Projekten auf der ganzen Welt bewiesen. Wir sind ein in Barcelona ansässiges Architekturbüro mit 40 Jahren internationaler Erfahrung in der Welt der architektonischen Gestaltung und Pioniere der Green Architecture. Die kulturellen, sozialen, landschaftlichen und ökologischen Werte des Territoriums werden in unsere Architektur integriert, um den Erfolg bei der Interpretation der Erwartungen und Anforderungen unserer Kunden zu garantieren. Wir verstehen architektonisches Design als ein Werkzeug zur Veränderung und Verbesserung der Gesellschaft. Unsere Projekte werden mit einer globalen und integrierten architektonischen Vision entworfen, die die Disziplinen Architektur, Innenarchitektur und Landschaftsdesign miteinander verbindet. Unser architektonisches Design erzeugt eine Wirkung durch Schönheit und Funktionalität, so dass Funktion und Emotion in Harmonie existieren.

ESTUDIO ARCHITECTS

BC Estudio Arquitectos, fondé par Javier Barba, est une solide équipe de professionnels de différentes nationalités qui partagent une vision et une méthode de conception qui caractérisent le cabinet depuis ses origines, avec d'excellents résultats, comme en témoignent les projets réalisés dans le monde entier. Nous sommes un cabinet d'architectes situé à Barcelone, fort de 40 ans d'expérience internationale dans le monde de la conception architecturale et pionnier de l'architecture verte. Les valeurs culturelles, sociales, paysagères et environnementales du territoire sont intégrées dans notre architecture afin de garantir le succès de l'interprétation des attentes et des exigences de nos clients. Nous comprenons la conception architecturale comme un outil permettant de changer et d'améliorer la société. Nos projets sont conçus avec une vision architecturale globale et intégrée, mêlant les disciplines de l'architecture, de la décoration intérieure et de l'aménagement paysager. Notre conception architecturale crée un impact par la beauté et la fonctionnalité, de sorte que la fonction et l'émotion existent en harmonie.

BC Estudio Arquitectos, fundado por Javier Barba, es un sólido equipo de profesionales de diferentes nacionalidades que comparten una visión y un método de diseño que han caracterizado a la firma desde sus orígenes, con excelentes resultados, como se ha demostrado en proyectos de todo el mundo. Somos un estudio de arquitectura ubicado en Barcelona con 40 años de experiencia internacional en el mundo del diseño arquitectónico y pioneros en Green Architecture. Los valores culturales, sociales, paisajísticos y ambientales del territorio se integran en nuestra arquitectura para garantizar el éxito en la interpretación de las expectativas y requerimientos de nuestros clientes. Entendemos el diseño de arquitectura como una herramienta para cambiar y mejorar la sociedad. Nuestros proyectos se diseñan con una visión arquitectónica global e integrada, mezclando las disciplinas de arquitectura, diseño de interiores y diseño de paisaje. Nuestro diseño arquitectónico crea un impacto por su belleza y funcionalidad, de manera que función y emoción existen en armonía.

The Torres family requested to create a place to present the best wines of their vineyard. From the outset it was clear that besides the technical aspects, the programs should display the spirit and emotion of the wine, without falling into a theatrical design. The project is divided into three levels, respecting the natural elevation of the land. The first underground level is where the barrels of wine are held in reserve. The second is developed as a cloister. This is a space for meditation and reflection that includes a fountain in the center. The transparent glass bottom of the fountain connects the center of the courtyard with the center of the underground plaza with a beam of light, symbolizing the union between the interior and exterior of the land. The third level houses a tasting room and museum, which are surrounded by water and linked to the atrium by a waterfall.

La famille Torres a demandé à créer un lieu pour présenter les meilleurs vins de leur vignoble. Dès le début, il était clair qu'en plus des aspects techniques, les programmes devaient montrer l'esprit et l'émotion du vin, sans tomber dans une conception théâtrale. Le projet est divisé en trois niveaux respectant l'élévation naturelle du terrain. Le premier niveau souterrain est celui où sont conservés les tonneaux de vin. Le deuxième niveau est développé sous la forme d'un cloître. C'est un espace de méditation et de réflexion qui comprend une fontaine au centre. Le fond en verre transparent de la fontaine relie le centre de la cour au centre de la place souterraine par un faisceau de lumière, symbolisant l'union entre l'intérieur et l'extérieur de la terre. Le troisième niveau abrite une salle de dégustation et un musée, entourés d'eau et reliés à l'atrium par une cascade.

Die Familie Torres hatte den Wunsch, einen Ort zu schaffen, an dem sie die besten Weine aus ihrem Weingut präsentieren kann. Von Anfang an war klar, dass die Programme neben den technischen Aspekten auch den Geist und die Emotionen des Weines zeigen sollten, ohne in ein theatralisches Design zu verfallen. Das Projekt ist in drei Ebenen unterteilt, die die natürliche Höhenlage des Geländes respektieren. Im ersten Untergeschoss werden die Weinfässer aufbewahrt. Die zweite Ebene ist in Form eines Kreuzganges ausgebaut. Es ist ein Raum für Meditation und Reflexion, der einen Brunnen in der Mitte beinhaltet. Der transparente Glasboden des Brunnens verbindet das Zentrum des Hofes mit dem Zentrum des unterirdischen Platzes mit einem Lichtstrahl, der die Vereinigung zwischen dem Inneren und der äußeren Erde symbolisiert. Die dritte Ebene beherbergt einen Verkostungsraum und ein Museum, das von Wasser umgeben und durch einen Wasserfall mit dem Atrium verbunden ist.

La familia Torres solicitó crear un lugar para presentar los mejores vinos de su viñedo. Desde el principio estaba claro que, además de los aspectos técnicos, los programas debían mostrar el espíritu y la emoción del vino, sin caer en un diseño teatral. El proyecto se divide en tres niveles respetando la elevación natural del terreno. El primer nivel subterráneo es donde se reservan las barricas de vino. El segundo se desarrolla en forma de claustro. Se trata de un espacio de meditación y reflexión que incluye una fuente en el centro. El fondo de cristal transparente de la fuente conecta el centro del patio con el centro de la plaza subterránea con un haz de luz, simbolizando la unión entre el interior y la tierra exterior. El tercer nivel alberga una sala de degustación y un museo, rodeados de agua y unidos al atrio por una cascada.

Located a short walk from The Arcade (first project of BC for this winery), the building presents a series of spaces that bring the world of wine closer to visitors. You can access it across a square, and going through a large doorway. A lobby allows to view the various activities carried out: the private and groups tastings rooms and on the back, the service areas, which support the events organization. The tasting room, with a bar that has as its backdrop the magnificent landscape of the vast fields of vineyards and mountains, allows the visitor to taste the wine with a stimulating and panoramic view. This indoor-outdoor feeling is enhanced in architectural terms by the actual amount of space, defined by thick stone walls, wooden ceiling, and the carpentry with large windows from floor to ceiling.

Situé à deux pas de The Arcade (premier projet de BC pour ce domaine viticole), le bâtiment présente une série d'espaces qui rapprochent le monde du vin des visiteurs. On y accède par une place, par une grande porte. Un foyer offre une vue sur les différentes activités qui s'y déroulent : les salles de dégustation privées et collectives et, à l'arrière, les zones de service, qui permettent l'organisation d'événements. La salle de dégustation, dotée d'un bar avec en toile de fond le magnifique paysage des vastes champs de vignes et des montagnes, permet au visiteur de déguster le vin avec une vue stimulante et panoramique. Cette sensation d'intérieur-extérieur est renforcée en termes architecturaux par la quantité réelle d'espace, définie par les épais murs de pierre, le plafond en bois et les boiseries avec de grandes fenêtres du sol au plafond.

Nur einen Steinwurf von The Arcade entfernt (BCs erstes Projekt für diese Weinkellerei), präsentiert das Gebäude eine Reihe von Räumen, die dem Besucher die Welt des Weins näher bringen. Der Zugang erfolgt über einen Platz, durch eine große Türöffnung. Ein Foyer gibt den Blick frei auf die verschiedenen Aktivitäten, die hier stattfinden: die privaten und Gruppenverkostungsräume und im hinteren Bereich die Servicebereiche, die die Organisation von Veranstaltungen unterstützen. Der Verkostungsraum mit einer Bar vor der herrlichen Kulisse der weitläufigen Weinbergsfelder und Berge ermöglicht es dem Besucher, den Wein mit einer anregenden und panoramischen Aussicht zu verkosten. Dieses Indoor-Outdoor-Gefühl wird architektonisch durch das tatsächliche Raumangebot verstärkt, das durch die dicken Steinwände, die Holzdecke und den Holzbau mit großen, raumhohen Fenstern definiert wird.

Situado a un paso de The Arcade (primer proyecto de BC para esta bodega), el edificio presenta una serie de espacios que acercan el mundo del vino a los visitantes. Se puede acceder a él a través de una plaza, atravesando un gran portal. Un vestíbulo permite ver las distintas actividades que se realizan: las salas de catas privadas y de grupos y, en la parte posterior, las zonas de servicio, que dan soporte a la organización de eventos. La sala de catas, con una barra que tiene como telón de fondo el magnífico paisaje de los extensos campos de viñedos y montañas, permite al visitante degustar el vino con una estimulante y panorámica vista. Esta sensación de interior-exterior se ve reforzada en términos arquitectónicos por la cantidad real de espacio, definida por las gruesas paredes de piedra, el techo de madera y la carpintería con grandes ventanales del suelo al techo.

STAG'S LEAP WINE CELLARS

NAPA VALLEY, CALIFORNIA, USA

The collaboration between the client and the architect resulted in a balanced and impressive project among the large trees and existing rocks. One objective was to define the finishes of the two areas that can be found in the underground path: the Round Room, crowned with a large vault and located in the intersection of several tunnels, and the Great Room, where special guests are received. The wine cellar also has five entrances or different doorways. The project was to present a solution for each of them. The Arcade, a porch-series of arches that connects, communicates and enables visitors to be under shelter throughout the entire route. The design unifies and frames the two access doors to the wine cellar, leading to the Great Room, the library and the adjacent area to the kitchen for events. Behind these rooms a labyrinth of tunnels can be accessed, the junction of which is the Round Room, where a Foucault pendulum recalls the passage of time.

La collaboration entre le client et l'architecte a donné lieu à un projet équilibré et impressionnant entre les grands arbres et les rochers existants. L'un des objectifs était de définir les finitions des deux zones situées dans le parcours souterrain : la Salle Ronde, couronnée par une grande voûte et située à l'intersection de plusieurs tunnels, et la Grande Salle, où sont reçus les invités spéciaux. Le domaine viticole possède également cinq entrées ou portails différents. Le projet consistait à présenter une solution pour chacun d'entre eux. L'Arcade, un porche d'arcades qui relie, communique et permet aux visiteurs d'être à l'abri tout au long de la visite. Le design unifie et encadre les deux portes d'accès à la cave, qui mènent à la grande salle, à la bibliothèque et à la zone adjacente à la cuisine pour les événements. Derrière ces pièces se trouve un labyrinthe de tunnels, dont le point de jonction est la salle ronde, où un pendule de Foucault nous rappelle le passage du temps.

Die Zusammenarbeit zwischen dem Kunden und dem Architekten führte zu einem ausgewogenen und beeindruckenden Projekt zwischen den großen Bäumen und den vorhandenen Felsen. Eines der Ziele war es, die Oberflächen der beiden Bereiche zu definieren, die in der unterirdischen Route zu finden sind: der Runde Saal, der von einem großen Gewölbe gekrönt wird und an der Kreuzung mehrerer Tunnel liegt, und der Große Saal, in dem besondere Gäste empfangen werden. Das Weingut hat außerdem fünf verschiedene Eingänge oder Portale. Das Projekt bestand darin, für jeden von ihnen eine Lösung zu präsentieren. Die Arkade, ein Bogengang, der verbindet, kommuniziert und es den Besuchern ermöglicht, während des gesamten Rundgangs unter Dach zu sein. Der Entwurf vereinheitlicht und rahmt die beiden Zugangstüren zum Keller, die in den Großen Saal, die Bibliothek und den an die Küche angrenzenden Bereich für Veranstaltungen führen. Hinter diesen Räumen befindet sich ein Tunnellabyrinth, dessen Knotenpunkt der Runde Raum ist, in dem ein Foucaultsches Pendel an den Lauf der Zeit erinnert.

La colaboración entre el cliente y el arquitecto dio como resultado un proyecto equilibrado entre los grandes árboles y las rocas existentes. Uno de los objetivos era definir los acabados de las dos zonas que se encuentran en el recorrido subterráneo: la Sala Redonda, coronada por una gran bóveda y situada en la intersección de varios túneles, y la Gran Sala, donde se recibe a los invitados especiales. La bodega también cuenta con cinco entradas o portales diferentes. El proyecto consistía en presentar una solución para cada una de ellas. La Arcada, un porche de arcos que conecta, comunica y permite a los visitantes estar a cubierto durante todo el recorrido. El diseño unifica y enmarca las dos puertas de acceso a la bodega, que conducen a la Gran Sala, la biblioteca y la zona adyacente a la cocina para eventos. Tras estas estancias se accede a un laberinto de túneles, cuyo punto de unión es la Sala Redonda, donde un péndulo de Foucault recuerda el paso del tiempo.

DELL'AGNOLO –

DELL'AGNOLO – KELDERER ARCHITEKTURBÜRO

WWW.DA-K.NET

> KELLEREI BOZEN WINERY

Architecture studio in Bozen (IT) founded in 2000 by Sylvia Dell'Agnolo and Egon Kelderer, that connects the development of the contemporary city and the conservation of the historical and artistic heritage. During the 20 years of activity, the studio has been involved in the design and construction management, focusing on the restored and refurbishment of historical and artistic heritage buildings and the redevelopment and renovation of the existing constructions with particular attention to energy saving and responsible use of resources. During this period residential, school and hotel buildings have been built. Particular interest has been addressed to the renovation of historic alpine farmhouses « masi ». Since 2008 the studio got interested in wineries architecture, winning competitions and prizes at an international level. The studio is active in Italy, Austria, Switzerland and Germany.

Architekturbüro in Bozen (IT), gegründet im Jahr 2000 von Sylvia Dell'Agnolo und Egon Kelderer, das die Entwicklung der zeitgenössischen Stadt und die Erhaltung des historischen und künstlerischen Erbes miteinander verbindet. In den 20 Jahren seiner Tätigkeit hat sich das Studio dem Design und der Bauleitung gewidmet, wobei es sich auf die Restaurierung und Sanierung historischer und kunsthistorischer Gebäude sowie auf den Umbau und die Renovierung bestehender Gebäude konzentriert und dabei besonderes Augenmerk auf Energieeinsparung und den verantwortungsvollen Umgang mit Ressourcen legt. In dieser Zeit wurden Wohn-, Schul- und Hotelbauten errichtet. Besonderes Augenmerk wurde auf die Renovierung historischer Bergbauernhäuser („masi") gelegt. Seit 2008 interessiert sich das Studio für die Architektur von Weingütern und gewann internationale Wettbewerbe und Auszeichnungen. Das Studio arbeitet in Italien, Österreich, der Schweiz und Deutschland.

KELDERER ARCHITEKTURBÜRO

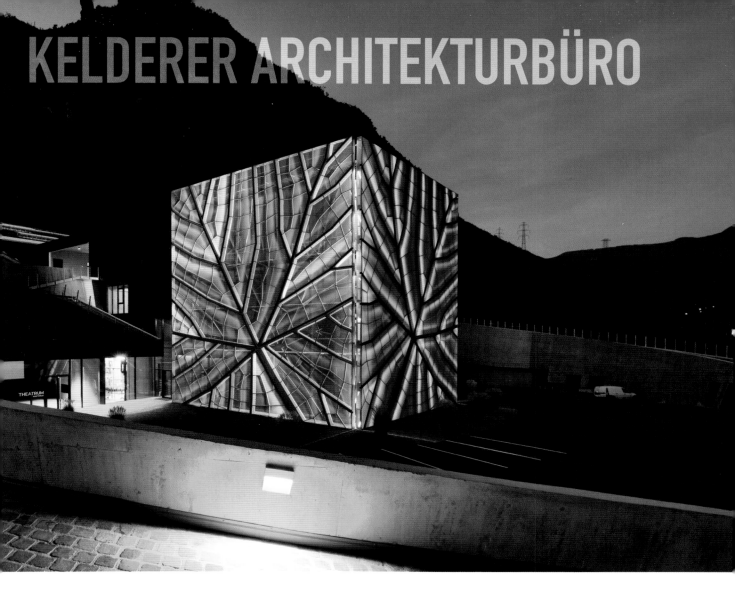

Studio d'architecture à Bozen (IT) fondé en 2000 par Sylvia Dell'Agnolo et Egon Kelderer, qui relie le développement de la ville contemporaine et la préservation du patrimoine historique et artistique. Tout au long de ses 20 ans d'activité, le studio s'est consacré à la conception et à la gestion de la construction, en se concentrant sur la restauration et la réhabilitation de bâtiments du patrimoine historique et artistique, ainsi que sur le remodelage et la rénovation de bâtiments existants, en accordant une attention particulière aux économies d'énergie et à l'utilisation responsable des ressources. Au cours de cette période, des bâtiments résidentiels, scolaires et hôteliers ont été construits. Un intérêt particulier a été accordé à la rénovation des fermes alpines historiques ("masi"). Depuis 2008, le studio s'est intéressé à l'architecture des vignobles, remportant des concours et des prix internationaux. Le studio travaille en Italie, en Autriche, en Suisse et en Allemagne.

Estudio de arquitectura de Bozen (IT) fundado en 2000 por Sylvia Dell'Agnolo y Egon Kelderer, que conecta el desarrollo de la ciudad contemporánea y la conservación del patrimonio histórico y artístico. A lo largo de sus 20 años de actividad, el estudio se ha dedicado al diseño y la gestión de la construcción, centrándose en la restauración y la rehabilitación de edificios del patrimonio histórico y artístico, así como en la remodelación y la renovación de las construcciones existentes, prestando especial atención al ahorro energético y al uso responsable de los recursos. Durante este periodo se han construido edificios residenciales, escolares y hoteleros. Se ha prestado especial interés a la renovación de masías históricas alpinas ("masi"). Desde 2008 el estudio se interesó por la arquitectura de bodegas, ganando concursos y premios a nivel internacional. El estudio trabaja en Italia, Austria, Suiza y Alemania.

The project was selected in a competition. The urbanistic focus was laid on integrating the large volume into the unique landscape while meeting all the innovative and necessary technical requirements of a modern winery. Furthermore, the visibility of the renowned winery was to be increased. The realized construction project represents the architectural result of an intensive investigation of the functional needs, that an energy-saving yet quality-enhancing production of wine in the "free-fall"-technique require nowadays. It was a physical consideration to dispense all pumps from the process. Pumping the pressed liquids would result in quality losses throughout the production. This is why every step from delivery of the grapes to storage and bottling has to be aligned in a vertical order. The winery consists of a symmetrical courtyard with the main administration and retail building in its center.

Le projet a été sélectionné dans le cadre d'un concours. L'approche urbanistique s'est concentrée sur l'intégration du grand volume dans le paysage unique, tout en répondant à toutes les exigences techniques innovantes et nécessaires d'une cave moderne. En outre, la visibilité devait être accrue. Le projet de construction réalisé représente le résultat architectural d'une recherche intensive sur les exigences fonctionnelles de la production actuelle de vin en « chute libre », qui permet d'économiser de l'énergie et d'améliorer la qualité. L'une des considérations physiques était de se passer de toutes les pompes de traitement. Le pompage des liquides pressés entraînerait des pertes de qualité dans l'ensemble du processus de production. Par conséquent, chaque étape, de la livraison des raisins au stockage et à la mise en bouteille, doit suivre un ordre vertical. Le domaine viticole consiste en une cour symétrique avec, en son centre, le bâtiment principal d'administration et de vente au détail.

Das Projekt wurde im Rahmen eines Wettbewerbs ausgewählt. Der städtebauliche Ansatz konzentrierte sich auf die Integration des großen Volumens in die einzigartige Landschaft und erfüllte gleichzeitig alle innovativen und notwendigen technischen Anforderungen an ein modernes Weingut. Darüber hinaus musste die Sichtbarkeit erhöht werden. Das realisierte Bauprojekt stellt das architektonische Ergebnis einer intensiven Auseinandersetzung mit den funktionalen Anforderungen der heutigen energiesparenden und qualitätssteigernden Weinproduktion im „freien Fall" dar. Eine physikalische Überlegung war der Verzicht auf alle Prozesspumpen. Das Abpumpen der gepressten Flüssigkeiten würde zu Qualitätsverlusten im gesamten Produktionsprozess führen. Deshalb muss jeder Schritt, von der Anlieferung der Trauben bis zur Lagerung und Abfüllung, einer vertikalen Ordnung folgen. Das Weingut besteht aus einem symmetrischen Innenhof, in dessen Mitte sich das Hauptverwaltungs- und Verkaufsgebäude befindet.

El proyecto fue seleccionado en un concurso. El enfoque urbanístico se centró en la integración del gran volumen en el singular paisaje, al tiempo que se cumplían todos los requisitos técnicos innovadores y necesarios de una bodega moderna. Además, había que aumentar la visibilidad. El proyecto de construcción realizado representa el resultado arquitectónico de una intensa investigación de las necesidades funcionales que requiere hoy en día una producción de vino que ahorre energía y mejore la calidad en la técnica de "caída libre". Una consideración física fue prescindir de todas las bombas del proceso. El bombeo de los líquidos prensados provocaría pérdidas de calidad en toda la producción. Por ello, cada paso, desde la entrega de la uva hasta el almacenamiento y el embotellado, debe seguir un orden vertical. La bodega consta de un patio simétrico con el edificio principal de administración y venta al por menor en su centro.

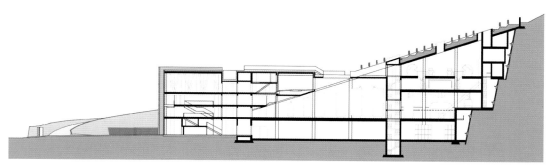

Section

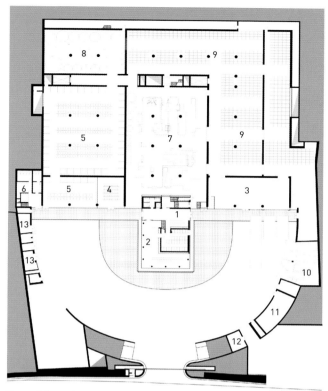

Ground floor plan

1. Entrance and reception
2. Sales area
3. Loading and unloading area
4. Auditorium
5. Wine-cellar
6. Locker room
7. Bottling plant
8. Wines racking and storage room
9. Bottles storage area
10. Waste storage
11. Retention basin
12. Storage room
13. Technical room

DESTILAT

WWW.DESTILAT.AT

> CLEMENS STROBL WINERY

The creative heads behind Destilat are Harald Hatschenberger, Thomas Neuber and Henning Weimer. Destilat is nationally and internationally active in interior design and furniture design and maintains offices in Vienna and Linz.

Destilat is developing architectural concepts for private and corporate customers. Each project is seen in a holistic context and offers comprehensive, elaborate interior concepts, paying careful attention even to the smallest details.

Die kreativen Köpfe von Destilat sind Harald Hatschenberger, Thomas Neuber und Henning Weimer. Destilat ist national und international auf dem Gebiet der Innenarchitektur und des Möbeldesigns tätig und hat Büros in Wien und Linz.

Destilat entwickelt Architekturkonzepte für Privat- und Firmenkunden. Jedes Projekt wird in einem ganzheitlichen Kontext gesehen und bietet komplette und durchdachte Einrichtungskonzepte mit Aufmerksamkeit für jedes noch so kleine Detail.

DESTILAT

Les responsables de la création de Destilat sont Harald Hatschenberger, Thomas Neuber et Henning Weimer. Destilat est actif au niveau national et international dans le domaine de l'architecture d'intérieur et du design de mobilier et possède des bureaux à Vienne et à Linz.

Destilat développe des concepts architecturaux pour des clients privés et des entreprises. Chaque projet est considéré dans un contexte global et offre des concepts d'aménagement intérieur complets et élaborés, en prêtant attention aux moindres détails.

Las cabezas creativas de Destilat son Harald Hatschenberger, Thomas Neuber y Henning Weimer. Destilat desarrolla su actividad a nivel nacional e internacional en el ámbito del diseño de interiores y del mobiliario, y tiene oficinas en Viena y Linz.

Destilat desarrolla conceptos arquitectónicos para clientes privados y corporativos. Cada proyecto se contempla en un contexto holístico y ofrece conceptos de interiorismo completos y elaborados, prestando atención incluso a los detalles más pequeños.

The Clemens Strobl winery is the economic heart of the facilities surrounding the former 19th century Meierhof of Schloss Winklberg in Mitterstockstall am Wagarm. It comprises a wine cellar with original vaults, a new tasting room with a kitchen as well as offices. These business premises consist of two long gabled houses, which meet in an obtuse angle, one of them a gutted and extensively restored original, the other a newer building that replaced a barn that was "beyond saving". The connecting element of the two buildings is a steel construction that tapers towards the inner courtyard and refers to long past days of industrial architecture with its rungs. Below, the cubically inserted tasting room links the two buildings on the inside.

La cave Clemens Strobl est le cœur économique de l'installation entourant l'ancien Meierhof du 19e siècle du Schloss Winklberg à Mitterstockstall am Wagarm. Il comprend une cave avec des voûtes d'origine, une nouvelle salle de dégustation avec cuisine et des bureaux. Ces locaux commerciaux sont constitués de deux longues maisons à pignons, qui se rejoignent à un angle obtus, l'une étant l'originale, démolie et largement restaurée, et l'autre un nouveau bâtiment qui a remplacé une grange irrécupérable. L'élément de liaison entre les deux bâtiments est une construction métallique qui se rétrécit vers la cour intérieure et qui, avec ses marches, rappelle l'époque révolue de l'architecture industrielle. En bas, la salle de dégustation insérée de façon cubique relie les deux bâtiments à l'intérieur.

Das Weingut Clemens Strobl ist das wirtschaftliche Herzstück der Anlagen rund um den ehemaligen Meierhof von Schloss Winklberg aus dem 19. Jahrhundert in Mitterstockstall am Wagarm. Es umfasst einen Keller mit originalen Gewölben, einen neuen Verkostungsraum mit Küche und Büros. Dieses Geschäftshaus besteht aus zwei langen Giebelhäusern, die in einem stumpfen Winkel miteinander verbunden sind. Das eine ist das Original, das abgerissen und umfassend restauriert wurde, das andere ein Neubau, der eine nicht mehr zu rettende Scheune ersetzte. Das verbindende Element zwischen den beiden Gebäuden ist eine Stahlkonstruktion, die sich zum Innenhof hin verjüngt und mit ihren Stufen an die vergangene Zeit der Industriearchitektur erinnert. Unten verbindet der kubisch eingefügte Verkostungsraum die beiden Gebäude im Inneren.

La bodega Clemens Strobl es el corazón económico de las instalaciones que rodean el antiguo Meierhof del siglo XIX de Schloss Winklberg en Mitterstockstall am Wagarm. Comprende una bodega con bóvedas originales, una nueva sala de degustación con cocina y oficinas. Estos locales comerciales constan de dos largas casas a dos aguas, que se unen en un ángulo obtuso, una de ellas es la original, destruida y ampliamente restaurada, y la otra es un edificio nuevo que sustituyó a un granero insalvable. El elemento de unión de los dos edificios es una construcción de acero que se estrecha hacia el patio interior y que remite con sus peldaños a los tiempos pasados de la arquitectura industrial. Abajo, la sala de degustación insertada cúbicamente une los dos edificios por el interior.

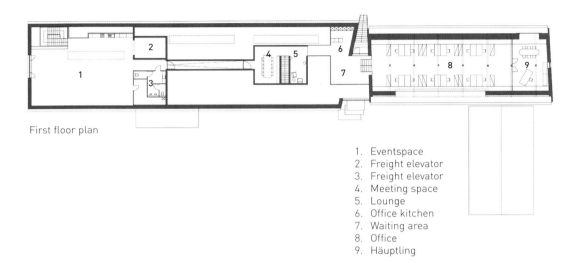

First floor plan

1. Eventspace
2. Freight elevator
3. Freight elevator
4. Meeting space
5. Lounge
6. Office kitchen
7. Waiting area
8. Office
9. Häuptling

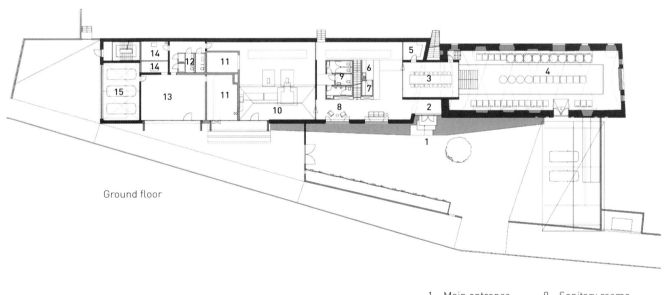

Ground floor

1. Main entrance
2. Entrance hall
3. Tasting room
4. Wine cellar
5. Vinotheque
6. Front desk/bar
7. Storage
8. Waiting area
9. Sanitary rooms
10. Wine delivery
11. Storage
12. Sanitary rooms
13. Vehicle space
14. Employee
15. Garage

DVA ARHITEKTA

WWW.DVA-ARHITEKTA.HR

> WINERY IN KUTJEVO

'Dva arhitekta' (Cro. 'two architects') is an architectural studio founded in 1992 by Tomislav Curkovic and Zoran Zidaric. Their first projects dealt mostly with interior design made with a minimal budget and a lot of effort, but quickly gained great recognition. In time, their primary focus shifted from interiors to family houses, a category which Dva arhitekta have branded with their own recognizable signature. Spanning their 25 year long collaboration, they have been winners and nominees for the most important architectural awards in Croatia and lately abroad, in competitions like Cemex Awards, Wienerberger Brick Award and World Architecture Festival. Three years in a row they were shortlisted for The Plan magazine Awards culminating in last years' win with of The Wine Chateau project in the production category. Although Dva arhitekta have worked mostly in Croatia, their scope extends even further, fuelled by numerous features in architectural magazines and sites, international book publications and exhibitions.

„Dva arhitekta" (kro. „zwei Architekten") ist ein Architekturbüro, das 1992 von Tomislav Curkovic und Zoran Zidaric gegründet wurde. Ihre ersten Projekte drehten sich meist um Innenarchitektur, die mit einem minimalen Budget und viel Aufwand gemacht wurden, aber sie erlangten bald große Anerkennung. Im Laufe der Zeit verlagerte sich ihr Schwerpunkt von Innenräumen auf Familienhäuser, eine Kategorie, für die sich Dva arhitekta erkennbar entschieden hat. In den 25 Jahren ihrer Zusammenarbeit waren sie Gewinner und Nominierte für die wichtigsten Architekturpreise in Kroatien und in letzter Zeit auch im Ausland, bei Wettbewerben wie den Cemex Awards, dem Wienerberger Brick Award und dem World Architecture Festival. Drei Jahre in Folge waren sie in der engeren Auswahl für die Auszeichnungen des Magazins The Plan, und im letzten Jahr gewannen sie das Projekt The Wine Chateau in der Kategorie Produktion. Obwohl Dva arhitekta in erster Linie in Kroatien gearbeitet hat, reicht ihre Reichweite weiter, was durch zahlreiche Artikel in Architekturmagazinen und -seiten, internationale Buchveröffentlichungen und Ausstellungen untermauert wird.

ARHITEKTA

« Dva arhitekta » (cro. « deux architectes ») est un bureau d'architecture fondé en 1992 par Tomislav Curkovic et Zoran Zidaric. Leurs premiers projets portaient principalement sur la décoration intérieure et étaient réalisés avec un budget minimal et beaucoup d'efforts, mais ils ont rapidement acquis une grande reconnaissance. Au fil du temps, leur objectif principal s'est déplacé de l'intérieur vers les maisons familiales, une catégorie à laquelle Dva arhitekta a adhéré de manière reconnaissable. Tout au long de leurs 25 années de collaboration, ils ont été lauréats et nominés pour les prix d'architecture les plus importants en Croatie et, dernièrement, à l'étranger, dans des concours tels que les Cemex Awards, le Wienerberger Brick Award et le World Architecture Festival. Ils ont été sélectionnés pour les prix du magazine The Plan et, l'année dernière, ils ont remporté le projet The Wine Chateau dans la catégorie production. Bien que Dva arhitekta ait travaillé principalement en Croatie, sa portée s'étend au-delà, alimentée par de nombreux articles dans des magazines et des pages d'architecture, des publications de livres internationaux et des expositions.

"Dva arhitekta" (cro. "dos arquitectos") es un estudio de arquitectura fundado en 1992 por Tomislav Curkovic y Zoran Zidaric. Sus primeros proyectos trataban sobre todo de diseño de interiores realizados con un presupuesto mínimo y mucho esfuerzo, pero pronto obtuvieron un gran reconocimiento. Con el tiempo, su enfoque principal pasó de los interiores a las casas familiares, una categoría que Dva arhitekta ha firmado de forma reconocible. A lo largo de sus 25 años de colaboración, han sido ganadores y nominados a los premios de arquitectura más importantes de Croacia y, últimamente, del extranjero, en certámenes como los Premios Cemex, el Premio Wienerberger Brick y el Festival Mundial de Arquitectura. Durante tres años consecutivos fueron preseleccionados para los premios de la revista The Plan, y el año pasado ganaron el proyecto The Wine Chateau en la categoría de producción. Aunque Dva arhitekta ha trabajado sobre todo en Croacia, su alcance se extiende más allá, alimentado por numerosos artículos en revistas y páginas de arquitectura, publicaciones de libros internacionales y exposiciones.

Winery Galić lays in croatian Slavonia, where the monks in 13th century founded the first abbey and wine cellar. The winery is placed in the Kutjevo city main street, and therefore primarily experienced as a city house. Only upon entering, one discovers a production facility. Clear architectonic design derives from the idea that the house fits into the city structure and yet remains contemporary. Initial inspiration comes from the traditional wine cellars and houses of the area, with concrete bases and brick walls that gain patina and robustness in time. The winery is divided in two parts; base in concrete vaults which comprises wine ageing in barrels and degustation area. The upper part of the house in brick holds the wine production, and communicates via back street. Contrary to the usual winery scheme, barrels are placed into the street window to have contact with the street and invite inside.

Le domaine viticole Galic est situé en Slavonie croate, où des moines ont fondé la première abbaye et le premier domaine viticole au 13e siècle. Il est situé dans la rue principale de la ville de Kutjevo, ressemblant à une maison dans la ville même. Ce n'est qu'en entrant que l'on découvre l'usine de production. La conception architecturale claire découle de l'idée que la maison s'intègre dans la structure de la ville tout en restant contemporaine. L'inspiration initiale vient des caves et des maisons traditionnelles de la région, avec des bases en béton et des murs en briques qui gagnent en patine et en robustesse avec le temps. La cave est divisée en deux parties : la cave souterraine voûtée en béton qui contient le vieillissement du vin en fûts et la zone de dégustation. La partie supérieure, en brique, abrite la production de vin, et est communiquée par la rue arrière. Contrairement à la disposition habituelle des établissements vinicoles, les barriques sont placées dans la fenêtre de la rue pour avoir un contact avec l'extérieur.

Das Weingut Galic befindet sich im kroatischen Slawonien, wo Mönche im 13. Jahrhundert die erste Abtei und das erste Weingut gründeten. Es befindet sich an der Hauptstraße der Stadt Kutjevo und sieht aus wie ein Haus in der Stadt selbst. Erst wenn Sie eintreten, entdecken Sie die Produktionsanlage. Die klare architektonische Gestaltung entspringt der Idee, dass sich das Haus in die Struktur der Stadt einfügt und dennoch zeitgemäß bleibt. Die ursprüngliche Inspiration stammt von den traditionellen Weingütern und Häusern der Gegend, mit Betonsockeln und Ziegelwänden, die mit der Zeit Patina und Robustheit gewinnen. Die Weinkellerei ist in zwei Teile unterteilt: den unterirdischen Betongewölbekeller, in dem der Wein in Fässern reift, und den Verkostungsbereich. Der obere Teil, in Backstein, beherbergt die Weinproduktion und ist durch die Hinterstraße erschlossen. Entgegen dem üblichen Schema von Weingütern werden die Fässer im Fenster zur Straße hin aufgestellt, um Kontakt mit der Außenwelt zu haben.

La bodega Galic se encuentra en la Eslavonia croata, donde los monjes fundaron en el siglo XIII la primera abadía y bodega. Está situada en la calle principal de la ciudad de Kutjevo, pareciendo una casa de la propia ciudad. Sólo al entrar se descubre la planta de producción. El claro diseño arquitectónico se deriva de la idea de que la casa encaja en la estructura de la ciudad y, sin embargo, sigue siendo contemporánea. La inspiración inicial proviene de las bodegas y casas tradicionales de la zona, con bases de hormigón y paredes de ladrillo que ganan pátina y robustez con el tiempo. La bodega está dividida en dos partes; el subterráneo de bóvedas de hormigón que comprende la crianza del vino en barricas y la zona de degustación. La parte superior, en ladrillo, alberga la producción de vino, y se comunica a través de la calle trasera. En contra del esquema habitual de las bodegas, las barricas se colocan en la ventana de la calle para tener contacto con el exterior.

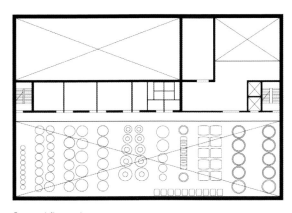

Second floor plan

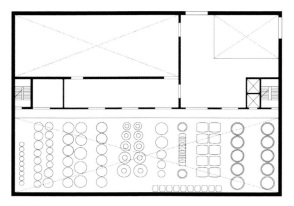

First floor plan

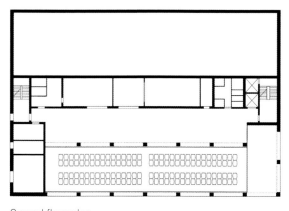

Ground floor plan

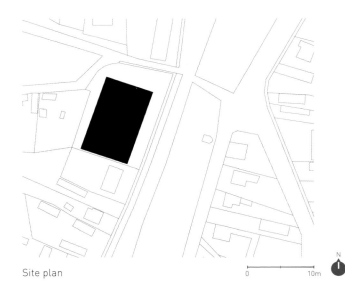

Site plan

0   10m

IDOM

WWW.IDOM.COM

> BODEGA BERONIA RIOJA
> BODEGA BERONIA RUEDA

Gonzalo Tello and Borja Gómez are architects and members of the IDOM team. They assume the role of Lead architects and project managers and have been the authors of the Beronia Rueda and Beronia Ollauri wineries.

IDOM Arquitectura is born from the illusion of those who want to be architects in the always fertile field of a multidisciplinary team. All this, with the aim of strengthening and respecting the skills and abilities of all the people involved, and also recognising the professional contribution of the unique individuals who make up the team. A complex balance of shared interests in an attempt to go further: to try to integrate and recognise the contributions of all.

IDOM's work can be understood as the result of a professional coexistence that respects the personality and singularity of its members and shares certain principles of action. These principles do not prevent the works from being conceived by authors and teams with their own personality and identity.

Gonzalo Tello und Borja Gómez sind Architekten und Mitglieder des IDOM-architekturteams. Sie übernehmen die Rolle des Projektmanagers und sind die Urheber der Weingüter Beronia Rueda und Beronia Ollauri gewesen.

IDOM arquitectura ist aus der Illusion derer entstanden, die Architekten im immer fruchtbaren Feld eines multidisziplinären Teams sein wollen. All dies mit dem Ziel, die Fähigkeiten und Fertigkeiten aller Beteiligten zu fördern und zu respektieren und auch den professionellen Beitrag der einzigartigen Individuen, die es ausmachen, anzuerkennen. Ein komplexes Gleichgewicht gemeinsamer Interessen in einem Versuch, weiter zu gehen: zu versuchen, die Beiträge aller zu integrieren und anzuerkennen.

Die Arbeit von IDOM kann als Ergebnis eines professionellen Miteinanders verstanden werden, das die Persönlichkeit und Einzigartigkeit der Mitglieder respektiert und bestimmte Handlungsprinzipien teilt. Diese Grundsätze schließen nicht aus, dass die Werke von Autoren und Teams mit eigener Persönlichkeit und Identität konzipiert werden.

IDOM

Gonzalo Tello et Borja Gómez sont architectes et membres de l'équipe d'architecture d'IDOM. Ils assument le rôle de chefs de projet et ont été les auteurs des caves Beronia Rueda et Beronia Ollauri.

IDOM Arquitectura est né de l'illusion de ceux qui veulent être architectes dans le domaine toujours fertile d'une équipe multidisciplinaire. Tout cela, dans le but de valoriser et de respecter les compétences et les capacités de toutes les personnes impliquées, mais aussi de reconnaître la contribution professionnelle des individus uniques qui la composent. Un équilibre complexe d'intérêts partagés dans une tentative d'aller plus loin : essayer d'intégrer et de reconnaître les contributions de tous.

Le travail d'IDOM peut être compris comme le résultat d'une coexistence professionnelle qui respecte la personnalité et la singularité de ses membres et partage certains principes d'action. Ces principes n'empêchent pas les œuvres d'être conçues par des auteurs et des équipes ayant leur propre personnalité et identité.

Gonzalo Tello y Borja Gómez son arquitectos y miembros del equipo de arquitectura de IDOM. Asumen el rol de directores de proyecto y han sido los autores de las bodegas Beronia Rueda y Beronia Ollauri.

IDOM arquitectura se gesta desde la ilusión de quien pretende ser arquitecto en el campo siempre fértil de un equipo multidisciplinar. Todo ello, con el ánimo de potenciar y respetar las capacidades y habilidades de todas las personas intervinientes, y reconociendo además la aportación profesional de los individuos singulares que lo conforman. Un complejo equilibrio de intereses compartidos en un intento por llegar más lejos: tratar de integrar y reconocer las aportaciones de todos.

El trabajo de IDOM se puede entender como el resultado de una convivencia profesional que respeta la personalidad y singularidad de sus miembros y comparte algunos principios de acción. Estos principios no impiden que las obras sean concebidas por autores y equipos con personalidad e identidad propia.

PHOTOS © FRANCESCO PINTÓN, MANUEL BOUZAS

Located in the Rioja Alta, in the north of Spain, the landscape of vineyards in which the winery is set is so powerful that we proposed to give it the leading role. We used gravity and geometry to increase the efficiency of the process and adapt to the topography and geology. We deploy the form factor to increase ground contact by controlling temperature and reduce the façade to a minimum. The geometrical, topographical, functional, constructive, energetic and productive operation have been conceived as a unit and are deeply linked to the site in physical terms. The activated concrete slabs and the 11 geothermal wells make the winery take root in the earth and participate in its cycles, resulting in a respectful exchanger between nature and the final product, the wine. It takes and gives off energy alternately in summer and winter, in an annual balance made possible by its implementation and geometry.

Situé dans la Rioja Alta, au nord de l'Espagne, le paysage de vignobles dans lequel s'inscrit la cave est si puissant que nous avons proposé de lui donner le rôle principal. Nous avons utilisé la gravité et la géométrie pour accroître l'efficacité du processus et nous adapter à la topographie et à la géologie. Nous déployons le facteur de forme pour augmenter le contact avec le sol en contrôlant la température et réduire la façade au minimum. L'opération géométrique, topographique, fonctionnelle, constructive, énergétique et productive a été conçue comme une unité et est profondément liée au site en termes physiques. Les dalles en béton activé et les 11 puits géothermiques font que la cave s'enracine dans la terre et participe à ses cycles, ce qui se traduit par un échange respectueux entre la nature et le produit final, le vin. Il prend et donne de l'énergie alternativement en été et en hiver, dans un équilibre annuel rendu possible par son implantation et sa géométrie.

In der Rioja Alta, im Norden Spaniens, gelegen, ist die Landschaft der Weinberge, in die das Weingut eingebettet ist, so eindrucksvoll, dass wir vorgeschlagen haben, ihr die Hauptrolle zu geben. Wir nutzten die Schwerkraft und die Geometrie, um die Effizienz des Prozesses zu erhöhen und uns an die Topografie und Geologie anzupassen. Wir setzen den Formfaktor ein, um den Kontakt mit dem Boden durch die Steuerung der Temperatur zu erhöhen und die Fassade auf ein Minimum zu reduzieren. Der geometrische, topographische, funktionale, konstruktive, energetische und produktive Betrieb wurde als Einheit konzipiert und ist physisch eng mit dem Ort verbunden. Die aktivierten Betonplatten und die 11 geothermischen Brunnen lassen das Weingut in der Erde verwurzeln und an ihren Zyklen teilhaben, was zu einem respektvollen Austausch zwischen der Natur und dem Endprodukt, dem Wein, führt. Er nimmt und gibt Energie abwechselnd im Sommer und im Winter, in einem jährlichen Gleichgewicht, das durch seine Einpflanzung und Geometrie ermöglicht wird.

Ubicado en la Rioja Alta, en el norte de España, el paisaje de viñedos en el que se enclava la bodega es tan potente que propusimos cederle el protagonismo. Utilizamos la gravedad y geometría para incrementar la eficiencia del proceso y adaptarnos a la topografía y geología. Desplegamos el factor de forma para incrementar el contacto con el terreno controlando la temperatura y reducimos la fachada al mínimo. La operación geométrica, topográfica, funcional, constructiva, energética y productiva han sido concebidas como unidad y están profundamente ligadas al lugar en términos físicos. Las losas de hormigón activadas y los 11 pozos de geotermia hacen que la bodega enraíce en la tierra y participe de sus ciclos, resultando en un intercambiador respetuoso entre la naturaleza y el producto final, el vino. Toma y cede energía alternativamente en verano e invierno, en un equilibrio anual posible por su implantación y geometría.

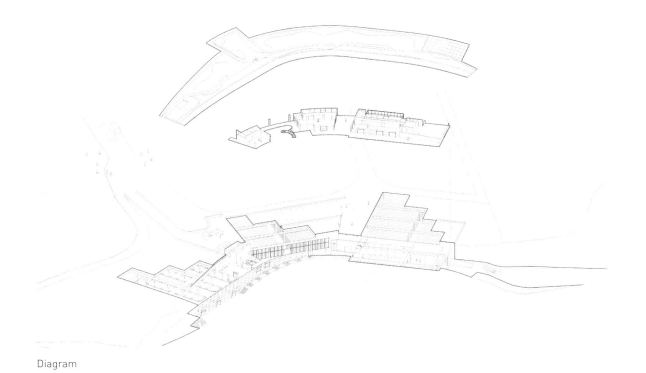

Diagram

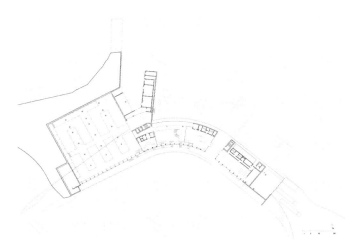

First floor plan

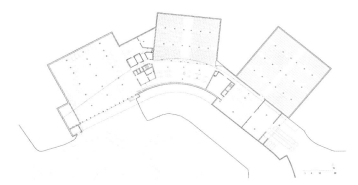

Ground floor plan

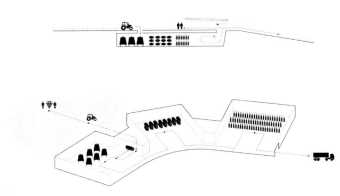

Operating diagram

The new winery, in addition to meeting the needs of white wine production by incorporating the latest advances and technologies in the field of oenology, had to respond to a wine tourism programme and generate an attractive image.

The winemaking area is conceived as a unitary space that revolves around a central nucleus presided over by a sculptural staircase and around which the laboratory, the barrel room and the tasting room are situated, with concrete tanks on one side and stainless steel tanks on the other.

The structure of the winery is made up of 6 porticoes of walls and large concrete beams that span 10 m over which are placed prefabricated TT slabs of up to 14 m in length. The latter are the ones that will give the interior space and exterior volume a unitary image, configuring the identity of the winery.

La nouvelle cave, en plus de répondre aux besoins de la production de vin blanc en intégrant les dernières avancées et technologies dans le domaine de l'œnologie, devait répondre à un programme d'œnotourisme et générer une image attractive.

La zone de vinification est conçue comme un espace unitaire qui tourne autour d'un noyau central présidé par un escalier sculptural et autour duquel se trouvent le laboratoire, la salle des tonneaux et la salle de dégustation, avec des cuves en béton d'un côté et des cuves en acier inoxydable de l'autre.

La structure de la cave est résolue au moyen de 6 portiques de murs et de grandes poutres en béton qui couvrent 10 m de lumière sur lesquels sont placées des dalles TT préfabriquées jusqu'à 14 m de longueur. Ce sont ces derniers qui donneront à l'espace intérieur et au volume extérieur une image unitaire, configurant l'identité de la cave.

Die neue Weinkellerei sollte nicht nur die Bedürfnisse der Weißweinproduktion erfüllen, indem sie die neuesten Fortschritte und Technologien auf dem Gebiet der Önologie einbezieht, sondern auch auf ein Weintourismusprogramm reagieren und ein attraktives Image erzeugen.

Der Weinherstellungsbereich ist als einheitlicher Raum konzipiert, der sich um einen zentralen Kern dreht, der von einer skulpturalen Treppe überragt wird und um den sich das Labor, der Fassraum und der Verkostungsraum befinden, mit Betontanks auf der einen und Edelstahltanks auf der anderen Seite.

Die Struktur der Weinkellerei wird durch 6 Portikus aus Mauern und großen Betonbalken gelöst, die 10 m Licht überspannen, auf denen vorgefertigte TT-Platten bis zu 14 m Länge platziert sind. Letztere sind es, die dem Innenraum und dem Außenvolumen ein einheitliches Bild geben und die Identität des Weinguts konfigurieren.

La nueva bodega, además de atender las necesidades de producción de vinos blancos incorporando los últimos avances y tecnologías en el campo de la enología, debía dar respuesta a un programa de enoturismo y generar una imagen atractiva.

La zona de elaboración se concibe como un espacio unitario que gira en torno a un núcleo central presidido por una escalera escultórica y en torno al que se sitúa el laboratorio, la sala de barricas y la sala de catas, quedando a un lado depósitos de hormigón y de acero inoxidable al otro.

La estructura de la bodega se resuelve mediante 6 pórticos de muros y grandes vigas de hormigón que salvan 10 m de luz sobre las que se sitúan unas placas prefabricadas TT de hasta 14 m de longitud. Estas últimas, son las que dotarán al espacio interior y volumen exterior de una imagen unitaria configurando la identidad de la bodega.

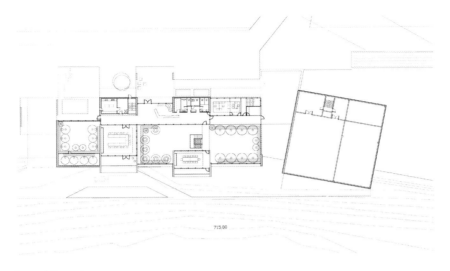

Ground floor plan

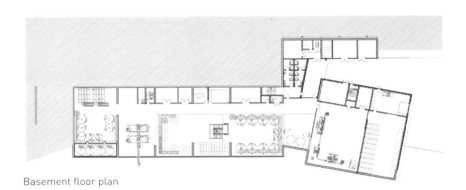

Basement floor plan

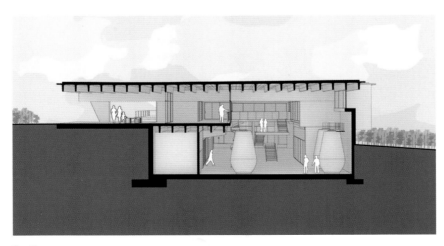

Section

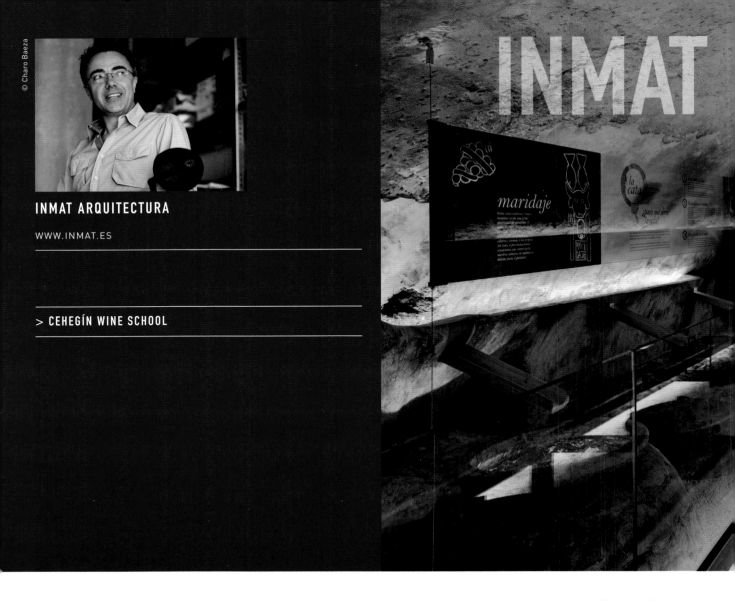

© Charo Baeza

INMAT ARQUITECTURA

WWW.INMAT.ES

> CEHEGÍN WINE SCHOOL

INMAT is made up of an outstanding team of professionals dedicated to the practice of architecture on a wide range of scales, from the design of objects as a specific product or as part of a complex system, to the residential and public sphere, developing projects adapted to specific needs. INMAT creatively investigates intelligent forms and methods, trying to discover, through analysis and reflection, new possibilities in the daily use of spaces and their socio-cultural implications. INMAT's work is above all personalised when dealing with residential spaces; with a markedly corporate character when related to the business or professional sphere; and especially strategic when dealing with public or planning projects. On the other hand, there are nowadays a number of areas that are increasingly influential in architecture itself that INMAT deals with rationally and objectively, such as new technologies associated with comfort, optimisation of resources and production costs.

INMAT besteht aus einem herausragenden Team von Fachleuten, die sich der Praxis der Architektur in einem breiten Spektrum von Maßstäben widmen, von der Gestaltung von Objekten als spezifisches Produkt oder als Teil eines komplexen Systems, bis hin zum Wohn- und öffentlichen Bereich, wobei Projekte entwickelt werden, die an spezifische Bedürfnisse angepasst sind. INMAT erforscht mit Kreativität, intelligenten Formen und Methoden und versucht durch Analyse und Reflexion neue Möglichkeiten in der täglichen Nutzung von Räumen und deren soziokulturelle Implikationen zu entdecken. Die Arbeit von INMAT ist vor allem individuell, wenn es um Wohnräume geht; mit ausgeprägtem Corporate-Charakter, wenn sie mit dem geschäftlichen oder professionellen Bereich zu tun haben; und besonders strategisch, wenn es um öffentliche oder planerische Projekte geht. Andererseits gibt es heute eine Reihe von zunehmend einflussreichen Bereichen in der Architektur selbst, mit denen sich INMAT rational und objektiv auseinandersetzt, wie z.B. neue Technologien im Zusammenhang mit Komfort, Ressourcenoptimierung und Produktionskosten.

ARQUITECTURA

INMAT est formé par une équipe exceptionnelle de professionnels qui se consacrent à la pratique de l'architecture à des échelles très diverses, de la conception d'objets en tant que produit spécifique ou en tant que partie d'un système complexe, à la sphère résidentielle et publique, en développant des projets adaptés à des besoins spécifiques. INMAT recherche à partir de la créativité, des formes et des méthodes intelligentes, en essayant de découvrir par l'analyse et la réflexion, de nouvelles possibilités dans l'utilisation quotidienne des espaces et leurs implications socio-culturelles. Le travail d'INMAT est avant tout personnalisé lorsqu'il s'agit d'espaces résidentiels ; avec un caractère corporatif marqué lorsqu'ils sont liés au domaine des affaires ou des professions libérales ; et surtout stratégique lorsqu'il s'agit de projets publics ou d'aménagement. D'autre part, il existe aujourd'hui une série de domaines de plus en plus influents dans l'architecture elle-même qu'INMAT traite de manière rationnelle et objective, comme les nouvelles technologies associées au confort, à l'optimisation des ressources et aux coûts de production.

INMAT está formado por un destacado equipo de profesionales dedicados a la práctica de la arquitectura en un amplio abanico de escalas, desde el diseño de objetos como producto específico o como parte de un sistema complejo, hasta el ámbito residencial y público, desarrollando proyectos adaptados a necesidades precisas. INMAT investiga desde la creatividad formas y métodos inteligentes, tratando de descubrir a través del análisis y la reflexión, nuevas posibilidades en el uso cotidiano de los espacios y en sus implicaciones socioculturales. El trabajo de INMAT es ante todo personalizado cuando se trata de espacios residenciales; con un marcado carácter corporativo cuando están relacionados con el ámbito empresarial o profesional; y especialmente estratégico cuando se trata de proyectos públicos o de planificación. Por otro lado, existen hoy en día una serie de áreas cada vez más influyentes en la propia arquitectura que INMAT aborda de forma racional y objetiva, como son las nuevas tecnologías asociadas al confort, la optimización de recursos y los costes de producción.

The old wine cellar where the project was developed belongs to an emblematic building called "Casa de la Tercia", which dates back to the 7th century. It is located on the semi-basement floor of the building. The purpose of the intervention project is to enhance the value of the building by developing an oenology school, exhibition space and museum for its visitors. In accordance with the project, we converted this interesting space into a gallery, with 342 m², where the main vault from the entrance is crossed by a glass ramp that descends gently before levelling out to become a glass carpet, a transparent and colourless walkway but full of fleeting reflections.

Conceptually, raw steel and wood are very elemental materials that work well with the historic parts of the interior, respecting the handcrafted character and patina of time.

L'ancienne cave où le projet a été développé appartient à un bâtiment emblématique appelé « Casa de la Tercia », qui date du 7e siècle. Il est situé au demi-sous-sol de l'immeuble. L'objectif du projet d'intervention est de le valoriser en développant une école d'œnologie, un espace d'exposition et un musée pour ses visiteurs. Conformément au projet, nous avons transformé cet espace intéressant en galerie, avec 342 m², où la voûte principale de l'entrée est traversée par une rampe en verre qui descend doucement avant de se niveler pour devenir un tapis de verre, une passerelle transparente et incolore mais pleine de reflets fugaces.

Conceptuellement, l'acier brut et le bois sont des matériaux très élémentaires qui s'accordent bien avec les parties historiques de l'intérieur, en respectant le caractère artisanal et la patine du temps.

Der alte Weinkeller, in dem das Projekt entwickelt wurde, gehört zu einem emblematischen Gebäude namens „Casa de la Tercia", das aus dem 7. Jahrhundert stammt. Es befindet sich im Halbuntergeschoss des Gebäudes. Der Zweck des Interventionsprojekts ist die Aufwertung des Ortes durch die Entwicklung einer Önologie-Schule, eines Ausstellungsraums und eines Museums für seine Besucher. In Übereinstimmung mit dem Projekt haben wir diesen interessanten Raum in eine Galerie mit 342 m² umgewandelt, in der das Hauptgewölbe vom Eingang aus von einer Glasrampe durchquert wird, die sanft abfällt, bevor sie sich zu einem Glasteppich abflacht, einem transparenten und farblosen Gang, aber voller flüchtiger Reflexionen.

Konzeptionell sind roher Stahl und Holz sehr elementare Materialien, die gut mit den historischen Teilen des Interieurs zusammenarbeiten und den handwerklichen Charakter und die Patina der Zeit respektieren.

La antigua bodega donde se desarrolló el proyecto pertenece a un edificio emblemático llamado "Casa de la Tercia", que data del siglo VII. Se encuentra en la planta semisótano del edificio. La finalidad del proyecto de intervención es la puesta en valor del mismo mediante el desarrollo de una escuela de enología, espacio expositivo y museo para sus visitantes. De acuerdo con el proyecto, convertimos este interesante espacio en una galería, con 342 m², donde la bóveda principal desde la entrada es atravesada por una rampa de cristal que desciende suavemente antes de nivelarse para convertirse en una alfombra de cristal, una pasarela transparente e incolora pero llena de reflejos fugaces.

Conceptualmente, el acero bruto y la madera son materiales muy elementales que funcionan bien con las partes históricas del interior, respetando el carácter artesanal y la pátina del tiempo.

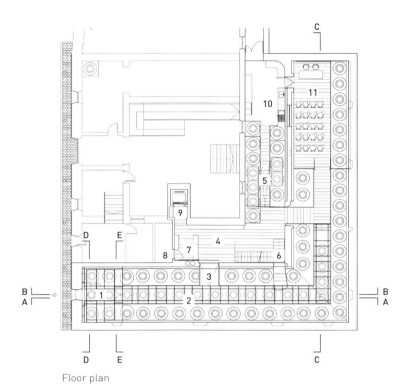

1. Access, windbreaks
2. Footbridge
3. Shop access
4. Shop
5. Tasting area
6. Staircase
7. Counter
8. Access to the plant room
9. Forklift access
10. Office
11. Classroom

Floor plan

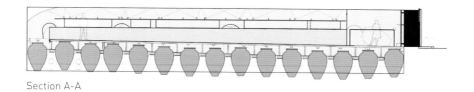

Section A-A

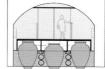

Section D-D

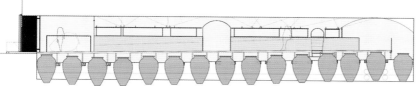

Section B-B

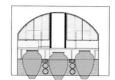

Section E-E

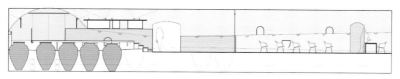

Section C-C

KAUNITZ YEUNG ARCHITECTURE

WWW.KAUNITZYEUNG.COM

> **RUNNING HORSE WINES**

KAUNITZ

Kaunitz Yeung Architecture is a multi-award winning, internationally recognised practice, founded by the husband and wife team of David Kaunitz and Ka Wai Yeung. It combines their extensive commercial experience with David's knowledge of living in and working with communities. The result is an architecture that places people at its centre and where good architecture does not need to necessarily be a luxury item. Their projects are bespoke solutions that sensitively respond to clients, stakeholders, end user requirements, site context and the budget.

Kaunitz Yeung Architecture ist ein mehrfach preisgekröntes und international anerkanntes Büro, das von dem Ehepaar David Kaunitz und Ka Wai Yeung gegründet wurde. Sie kombinieren ihre umfangreiche kommerzielle Erfahrung mit Davids Wissen über das Leben in und die Arbeit mit Gemeinden. Das Ergebnis ist eine Architektur, die den Menschen in den Mittelpunkt stellt und bei der gute Architektur kein Luxusgut sein muss. Ihre Projekte sind maßgeschneiderte Lösungen, die sensibel auf Kunden, Interessengruppen, Endbenutzeranforderungen, Standortkontext und Budget reagieren.

YEUNG ARCHITECTURE

Kaunitz Yeung Architecture est un cabinet primé à plusieurs reprises et reconnu au niveau international, fondé par le couple David Kaunitz et Ka Wai Yeung. Ils associent leur vaste expérience commerciale à la connaissance qu'a David de la vie dans les communautés et du travail avec elles. Le résultat est une architecture qui place les gens au centre et où une bonne architecture ne doit pas être un article de luxe. Ses projets sont des solutions sur mesure qui répondent de manière sensible aux clients, aux parties prenantes, aux exigences des utilisateurs finaux, au contexte du site et au budget.

Kaunitz Yeung Architecture es un estudio multipremiado y reconocido internacionalmente, fundado por el matrimonio David Kaunitz y Ka Wai Yeung. Combinan su amplia experiencia comercial con los conocimientos de David sobre la vida en las comunidades y el trabajo con ellas. El resultado es una arquitectura que sitúa a las personas en el centro y en la que la buena arquitectura no tiene por qué ser un artículo de lujo. Sus proyectos son soluciones a medida que responden con sensibilidad a los clientes, las partes interesadas, los requisitos del usuario final, el contexto del lugar y el presupuesto.

This project is a small, sensitive and almost temporary intervention into the landscape. The architectural expression of the shipping containers and steel structure reinforces the idea. Nestled in an existing stand of native trees, it required no trees to be removed and minimal contouring of the ground. The building is barely visible from the surrounding landscape, except for the reflection of the landscape in its large windows. Even the signage feels like a piece of rural equipment and not out of place. Highly insulated shipping containers and glass combine with the modest proportions to minimise energy use. The raw internal finish and minimal site works using stone from the vineyard minimised embodied energy. By making a modest, sensitive and easily removable intervention into the landscape, the sustainability of the landscape and vineyard has been maintained.

Ce projet est une petite intervention sensible et presque temporaire dans le paysage. L'expression architecturale des conteneurs maritimes et de la structure en acier renforce cette idée. Niché dans un peuplement d'arbres indigènes, aucun arbre n'a dû être abattu et le contour du site a été réduit au minimum. Le bâtiment est à peine visible de l'extérieur, si ce n'est par le reflet du paysage dans ses grandes fenêtres. Même la signalisation ressemble à une pièce d'équipement rural et n'est pas déplacée. Les conteneurs d'expédition hautement isolés et le verre se combinent aux proportions modestes pour minimiser la consommation d'énergie. La finition intérieure brute et les travaux minimaux réalisés avec la pierre du vignoble minimisent la consommation d'énergie. En effectuant une intervention modeste, sensible et facilement démontable dans le paysage, la durabilité du vignoble a été maintenue.

Dieses Projekt ist ein kleiner, sensibler und fast temporärer Eingriff in die Landschaft. Der architektonische Ausdruck der Schiffscontainer und der Stahlkonstruktion verstärkt die Idee. Eingebettet in einen einheimischen Baumbestand, mussten keine Bäume entfernt werden und die Kontur des Geländes wurde auf ein Minimum reduziert. Das Gebäude ist von außen kaum sichtbar, abgesehen von der Spiegelung der Landschaft in den großen Fenstern. Sogar die Beschilderung sieht aus wie ein ländliches Gerät und ist nicht deplatziert. Hochisolierte Schiffscontainer und Glas sorgen in Verbindung mit den bescheidenen Proportionen für einen minimalen Energiebedarf. Der rohe Innenausbau und die minimalen Arbeiten mit Steinen aus dem Weinberg minimieren den Energieverbrauch. Durch einen bescheidenen, sensiblen und leicht entfernbaren Eingriff in die Landschaft konnte die Nachhaltigkeit des Weinbergs erhalten werden.

Este proyecto es una intervención pequeña, sensible y casi temporal en el paisaje. La expresión arquitectónica de los contenedores de transporte y la estructura de acero refuerza la idea. Enclavado en una masa arbórea autóctona, no fue necesario retirar ningún árbol y el contorno del terreno fue mínimo. El edificio apenas es visible desde el exterior, salvo por el reflejo del paisaje en sus grandes ventanales. Incluso la señalización parece una pieza de equipamiento rural y no está fuera de lugar. Los contenedores de transporte altamente aislados y el vidrio se combinan con las modestas proporciones para minimizar el uso de energía. El acabado interior en bruto y las mínimas obras realizadas con piedra del viñedo minimizan el uso de energía. Al realizar una intervención modesta, sensible y fácilmente desmontable en el paisaje, se ha mantenido la sostenibilidad del viñedo.

MARKUS

MARKUS SCHERER

WWW.ARCHITEKTSCHERER.IT

> **DAS WEINDORF NALS**

Born in Vienna in 1962, he is an architect based in Italy who works in Merano and in Venice (1990) with V. Gregotti and B. D. Secchi. Since the start of his activity in 1992, his work has covered a wide range of themes, focusing on the revitalisation of listed buildings, cellars and exhibition designs. Through this diversity he achieves a synergistic connection between individual building tasks, such as the Landesmuseum Schloss Tirol, Festung Franzensfeste, the Palais Mamming Meran Museum, the Egyptian Collection Castello Sforzesco Milan, Stiftsplatz Kloster Neustift Vahrn, buildings for school and educational purposes as well as numerous wine cellars. A regular speaker and juror at architectural symposia, he has been lecturing at the FH Augsburg since 2014, at the University of Innsbruck since 2012 and at the Mozarteum Salzburg since 2018. He enjoys numerous publications, exhibition participations and awards, including the Venice Biennale, the *South Tyrol Architecture Prize* and the *Architetto Italiano* Prize for Building in Existing Contexts 2017.

1962 in Wien geboren, italienischer Architekt arbeitet in Meran, 1990 in Venedig bei V. Gregotti und B. Secchi promoviert. Seit Beginn seiner Tätigkeit im Jahr 1992 umfassen seine Arbeiten ein breites Spektrum an Thematiken mit Schwerpunkten in der Revitalisierung denkmalgeschützter Bauten, Weinkellereien und Ausstellungsgestaltungen. Durch diese Vielfältigkeit erreicht er eine synergetische Verbindung zwischen den einzelnen Bauaufgaben, wie Landesmuseum Schloss Tirol, Festung Franzensfeste, Museum Palais Mamming Meran, Ägyptische Sammlung Castello Sforzesco Mailand, Stiftsplatzes Kloster Neustift Vahrn, Gebäude für schulische und pädagogische Zwecke sowie zahlreiche Kellereien. Regelmäßig Referent und Juror in Architektursymposien, Lehrtätigkeit 2014 an der FH Augsburg, seit 2012 an der Universität Innsbruck sowie seit 2018 am Mozarteum in Salzburg. Zahlreiche Publikationen, Ausstellungsteilnahmen und Preise u.a. Biennale von Venedig, *Südtiroler Architekturpreis* und Preis *architetto italiano* für Bauen im Bestand 2017.

SCHERER

© Bruno Klomfar

Né à Vienne en 1962, il est un architecte basé en Italie qui travaille à Merano et à Venise (1990) avec V. Gregotti et B. D. Secchi. Depuis le début de son activité en 1992, son travail a couvert un large éventail de sujets, se concentrant sur la revitalisation de bâtiments classés, de domaines viticoles et de conceptions d'expositions. Grâce à cette diversité, il parvient à créer une synergie entre les différentes tâches de construction, comme le Landesmuseum Schloss Tirol, Festung Franzensfeste, le Palais Mamming Meran Museum, la collection égyptienne Castello Sforzesco Milan, Stiftsplatz Kloster Neustift Vahrn, les bâtiments scolaires et éducatifs ainsi que de nombreuses caves à vin. Régulièrement conférencier et juré lors de symposiums d'architecture, il donne des cours à la FH Augsburg en 2014, à l'université d'Innsbruck depuis 2012 et au Mozarteum Salzburg depuis 2018. Il bénéficie de nombreuses publications, participations à des expositions et récompenses, notamment la Biennale de Venise, le prix d'architecture du Tyrol du Sud et le prix *Architetto Italiano* pour la construction dans des contextes existants 2017.

Nacido en Viena en 1962, es un arquitecto radicado en Italia que trabaja en Merano y en Venecia (1990) con V. Gregotti y B. Doctorado Secchi. Desde el inicio de su actividad en 1992, su trabajo ha abarcado una amplia gama de temas, centrándose en la revitalización de edificios catalogados, bodegas y diseños de exposiciones. A través de esta diversidad logra una conexión sinérgica entre las tareas individuales de construcción, como el Landesmuseum Schloss Tirol, Festung Franzensfeste, el Museo Palais Mamming Meran, la Colección Egipcia Castello Sforzesco Milán, Stiftsplatz Kloster Neustift Vahrn, edificios para fines escolares y educativos, así como numerosas bodegas. Ponente y jurado habitual en simposios de arquitectura, imparte clases en la FH Augsburg en 2014, en la Universidad de Innsbruck desde 2012 y en el Mozarteum de Salzburgo desde 2018. Goza de numerosas publicaciones, participaciones en exposiciones y premios, entre ellos la Bienal de Venecia, el Premio de Arquitectura del Tirol del Sur y el Premio *Architetto Italiano* de Construcción en Contextos Existentes 2017.

The wine village of Nals lies at the foot of the Sirmian Hill. The consolidation of production in Nals in 2011 necessitated a complete redesign of the areas relevant to cellar technology. The newly conceived production process provides for the freely visible arrangement of the buildings in a wine yard. The result is a main building with a large cantilevered roof plate, a wine pressing tower, cellar rooms as well as a barrel cellar in wooden construction with a roof terrace for visitors. The building, made of reddish-brown fair-faced concrete, picks up the colour of the nearby rock walls and creates references to the landscape through chromaticism and materiality. In the course of the winery's constant quest for quality and the philosophy lived by the winery in synergy with the architecture, the historic heart of the winery will be carefully renovated in 2019 and the "Vinothek 1764" with presentation rooms and administrative headquarters will be rebuilt.

Le village viticole de Nals se trouve au pied de la colline de Sirmian. Le regroupement de la production à Nals en 2011 a nécessité un réaménagement complet des espaces relatifs à la technique de cave. Le processus de production nouvellement conçu prévoit la disposition librement visible des bâtiments dans une cour à vin. Le résultat est un bâtiment principal avec une grande plaque de toit en porte-à-faux, une tour de pressage du vin, des salles de cave ainsi qu'un chai à barriques en construction bois avec une terrasse sur le toit pour les visiteurs. Le bâtiment, réalisé en béton apparent de couleur rouge-brun, reprend la couleur des parois rocheuses voisines et crée des références au paysage par le chromatisme et la matérialité. Dans le cadre de la recherche constante de la qualité et de la philosophie vécue par la cave en synergie avec l'architecture, le cœur historique de la cave sera soigneusement rénové en 2019 et la « Vinothek 1764 » avec les salles de présentation et le siège administratif sera reconstruite.

Das Weindorf Nals liegt am Fuß des Sirmianer Hügels. Das Zusammenziehen der Produktion in Nals im Jahr 2011 erforderte die komplette Neugestaltung der kellertechnisch relevanten Bereiche. Der neu konzipierte Produktionsablauf sieht die frei einsichtige Anordnung der Baukörper in einen Weinhof vor. Entstanden ist ein Kopfgebäude mit weit austragender Dachplatte, Kelterturm, Kellerräumen sowie einen Barriquekeller in Holzbauweise mit Dachterrasse für Besucher. Der Bau aus rotbraunem Sichtbeton greift farblich die nahen Felswände auf und stellt durch Chromatik und Materialität Bezüge zur Landschaft her. Im Zuge des steten Strebens nach Qualität und der von Kellerei in Synergie mit der Architektur gelebten Philosophie wird im Jahr 2019 das historische Herz der Kellerei behutsam renoviert und die „Vinothek 1764" mit Präsentationsräumen und Verwaltungssitz umgebaut.

El pueblo vinícola de Nals se encuentra al pie de la colina de Sirmian. La consolidación de la producción en Nals en 2011 hizo necesario el rediseño completo de las áreas relevantes para la tecnología de las bodegas. El proceso de producción recién concebido prevé la disposición libremente visible de los edificios en un patio vinícola. El resultado es un edificio principal con una amplia placa de tejado en voladizo, una torre de prensado de vino, salas de bodega, así como una bodega de barricas en construcción de madera con una terraza en el tejado para los visitantes. El edificio, de hormigón visto de color marrón rojizo, recoge el color de las paredes rocosas cercanas y crea referencias al paisaje a través del cromatismo y la materialidad. En el curso de la búsqueda constante de la calidad y de la filosofía vivida por la bodega en sinergia con la arquitectura, el corazón histórico de la bodega será cuidadosamente renovado en 2019 y se reconstruirá la "Vinothek 1764" con salas de presentación y sede administrativa.

© Bruno Klomfar

© Helmuth Rier

© Bruno Klomfar

© Bruno Klomfar

© Bruno Klomfar

© Bruno Klomfar

© Bruno Klomfar

© Bruno Klomfar

© Bruno Klomfar

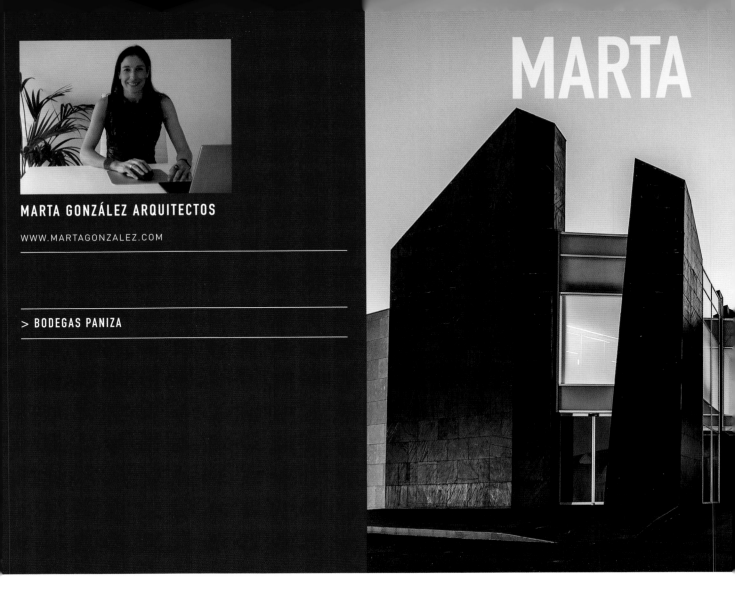

MARTA

MARTA GONZÁLEZ ARQUITECTOS

WWW.MARTAGONZALEZ.COM

> BODEGAS PANIZA

Marta González Alonso is an architect graduated from the ETSA of the University of Navarra. She began her professional activity in 1997 and in 2003 she started working in her studio in Madrid, founding Marta González Arquitectos.

The projects designed in the studio are customised for the end client for whom they are intended. They are projects with a large glazed surface area and with rounded volumes, which seek to achieve an exciting interior in each one of them, trying to improve the day-to-day life of the users through their architecture. This type of building is the studio's hallmark.

The projects include corporate and hotel architecture, as well as single-family homes and housing developments. These are custom-designed projects, adapted to the site on which they are located and seeking to be energy efficient, but mainly exciting and all this to meet the needs of each client, with whom we work in constant collaboration, pursuing their complete satisfaction.

Marta González Alonso ist Architektin an der ETSA der Universität von Navarra. Sie begann ihre berufliche Tätigkeit 1997 und 2003 gründete sie ihr Studio in Madrid, Marta González Arquitectos.

Die Projekte, die im Studio entworfen werden, sind für den Endkunden, für den sie bestimmt sind, personalisiert. Es handelt sich um Projekte mit einer großen verglasten Fläche und mit abgerundeten Volumina, die in jedem von ihnen ein aufregendes Interieur anstreben und versuchen, das tägliche Leben der Nutzer durch ihre Architektur zu verbessern. Diese Art von Gebäuden sind das Markenzeichen des Studios.

Bei den Projekten handelt es sich sowohl um Firmen- und Hotelarchitektur als auch um Einfamilienhäuser und Wohnsiedlungen. Es handelt sich um Projekte, die nach Maß entworfen werden, die an das Gelände, auf dem sie stehen, angepasst sind und die energieeffizient, aber vor allem aufregend sein sollen, und das alles, um die Bedürfnisse jedes einzelnen Kunden zu erfüllen, mit dem wir in ständiger Zusammenarbeit arbeiten und seine volle Zufriedenheit anstreben.

GONZÁLEZ ARQUITECTOS

Marta González Alonso est une architecte de l'ETSA de l'Université de Navarre. Elle a commencé son activité professionnelle en 1997 et en 2003, elle a commencé à travailler dans son studio à Madrid, en fondant Marta González Arquitectos.

Les projets qui sont conçus dans le studio sont personnalisés pour le client final auquel ils sont destinés. Il s'agit de projets présentant une grande surface vitrée et des volumes arrondis, qui cherchent à obtenir un intérieur passionnant dans chacun d'entre eux, en essayant d'améliorer la vie quotidienne des utilisateurs grâce à son architecture. Ce type de bâtiments est la marque de fabrique du studio.

Les projets développent aussi bien l'architecture d'entreprise et hôtelière que les maisons individuelles et les lotissements. Il s'agit de projets conçus sur mesure, adaptés au site sur lequel ils se trouvent et cherchant à être efficaces sur le plan énergétique, mais surtout passionnants et tout cela pour répondre aux besoins de chaque client, avec lequel nous travaillons en collaboration constante, à la recherche de leur entière satisfaction.

Marta González Alonso es arquitecto por la ETSA de la Universidad de Navarra. Inició su actividad profesional en 1997 y en 2003 comenzó a trabajar en su estudio en Madrid, fundando Marta González Arquitectos.

Los proyectos que se diseñan en el estudio están personalizados para el cliente final al que están destinados. Se trata de proyectos con una gran superficie acristalada y con volúmenes rotundos, que persiguen conseguir un interior emocionante en cada uno de ellos, tratando de mejorar el día a día de los usuarios a través de su arquitectura. Este tipo de edificios son la seña de identidad del estudio.

Los proyectos desarrollan tanto arquitectura corporativa y hotelera, como viviendas unifamiliares y en promoción. Se trata de proyectos diseñados a medida, adaptadas al solar en el que se asientan y buscando ser energéticamente eficientes, pero principalmente emocionantes y todo ello para cumplir con las necesidades de cada cliente, con el que se trabaja en colaboración constante, persiguiendo su completa satisfacción.

BODEGAS PANIZA

ZARAGOZA, SPAIN

The Paniza Wineries are designed based on the search to provide the wineries with a singular design space that is representative of their brand. Its geometric rotundity with volumes of broken shapes tries to transmit the singularity sought, to give strength to the design of its facilities.

The exterior volumes have been designed with a play of geometries and textures, all based on natural stone, both white and grey limestone and deep black slate. With accentuated geometries that are broken and cantilevered to enhance the effects of light on the different panels and that reflect what they house inside, being open with glazed surfaces of translucent glass curtain wall, with a slight degree of transparency that allows the perception of the exterior and interior.

La conception des établissements vinicoles de Paniza repose sur la recherche d'un espace de conception unique et représentatif de sa marque. Sa rotondité géométrique avec des volumes de formes brisées tente de transmettre la singularité recherchée, de donner de la force à la conception de ses installations.

Les volumes extérieurs ont été proposés avec des jeux géométriques et texturaux, tous basés sur la pierre naturelle, aussi bien le calcaire blanc et gris que l'ardoise noire intense. Avec des géométries accentuées, brisées et en porte-à-faux, pour renforcer les effets de la lumière sur les différents panneaux et refléter ce qu'ils abritent à l'intérieur, étant ouvert avec des surfaces vitrées de mur-rideau en verre translucide, avec un léger degré de transparence qui permet la perception de l'extérieur et de l'intérieur.

Das Design der Paniza Wineries basiert auf der Suche, den Weingütern einen einzigartigen Designraum zu bieten, der ihre Marke repräsentiert. Seine geometrische Rundung mit Volumina von gebrochenen Formen versucht, die gesuchte Einzigartigkeit zu vermitteln, um dem Design seiner Einrichtungen Kraft zu verleihen.

Die Außenvolumen wurden mit geometrischen und texturalen Spielen vorgeschlagen, die alle auf Naturstein basieren, sowohl auf weißem und grauem Kalkstein als auch auf intensivem schwarzem Schiefer. Mit akzentuierten Geometrien gebrochen und auskragend, um die Auswirkungen des Lichts auf die verschiedenen Platten zu verbessern und zu reflektieren, was sie im Inneren beherbergen, wobei offen mit verglasten Flächen aus transluzentem Glas Vorhangfassade, mit einem leichten Grad an Transparenz, die die Wahrnehmung der Außen-und Innenraum ermöglicht.

Las Bodegas Paniza están diseñadas partiendo de la búsqueda de dotar a las Bodegas de un espacio singular de diseño que sea representativo de su marca. Su rotundidad geométrica con volúmenes de formas quebradas trata de trasmitir la singularidad buscada, para otorgar fuerza al diseño de sus instalaciones.

Los volúmenes exteriores se han planteado con juegos de geometrías y texturas, todos ellos basados en piedra natural tanto de calizas blancas y grises como de pizarras de negro intenso. Con geometrías acentuadas quebradas y voladas, para potenciar los efectos de la luz sobre los diferentes paños y que reflejan lo que albergan en su interior, estando abiertas con superficies acristaladas de muro cortina de vidrio traslúcido, con un ligero grado de trasparencia que permite la percepción del exterior e interior.

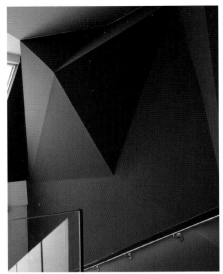

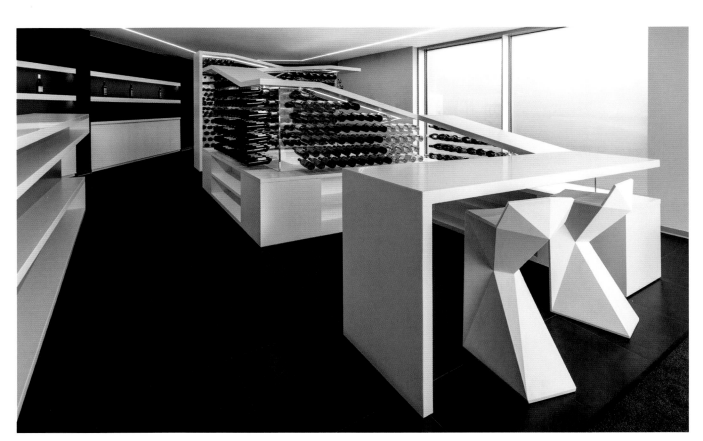

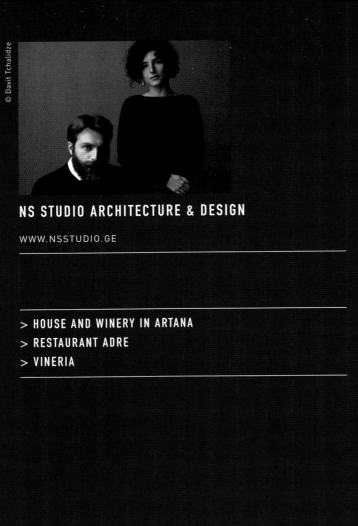

NS STUDIO ARCHITECTURE & DESIGN

WWW.NSSTUDIO.GE

> HOUSE AND WINERY IN ARTANA
> RESTAURANT ADRE
> VINERIA

NS STUDIO

NS STUDIO Architecture & Design was founded in 2013 by Luka Chaganava and Nino Tchanturia. Our goal is to create high-grade, interesting and original works in architecture and design. The portfolio of the studio includes projects of various types and scales, such as clinics, theatres, concert halls, hotels, multi-functional and business centers, residential houses and other commercial or private projects. Through these we strive to have a positive impact on the environment, space and people and to contribute to the proper development of architecture and design. Our team is staffed by professionals of all related specialties, and with their help we carry out full architecture and design projects; from our standpoint this is one of the most important prerequisites for turning the ideas into reality. We believe that it's vital to build up your own personality in this field, expressing the right context, content, functionality and individualism with each work; that makes our approach to the projects stand out.

NS STUDIO Architecture & Design wurde 2013 von Luka Chaganava und Nino Tchanturia gegründet. Unser Ziel ist es, qualitativ hochwertige, interessante und originelle Arbeiten in Architektur und Design zu schaffen. Das Portfolio des Studios umfasst Projekte verschiedener Arten und Größenordnungen, wie z.B. Kliniken, Theater, Konzertsäle, Hotels, Multifunktions- und Geschäftszentren, Wohnhäuser und andere kommerzielle oder private Projekte. Durch sie streben wir danach, einen positiven Einfluss auf die Umwelt, den Raum und die Menschen zu haben und zur richtigen Entwicklung von Architektur und Design beizutragen.
Unser Team besteht aus Fachleuten aller verwandten Spezialgebiete, mit deren Hilfe wir komplette Architektur- und Designprojekte realisieren; aus unserer Sicht eine der wichtigsten Voraussetzungen, um Ideen in die Realität umzusetzen. Wir glauben, dass es in diesem Bereich wichtig ist, eine eigene Persönlichkeit zu entwickeln, die mit jeder Arbeit den richtigen Kontext, den Inhalt, die Funktionalität und den Individualismus zum Ausdruck bringt; das zeichnet unsere Herangehensweise an Projekte aus.

ARCHITECTURE & DESIGN

NS STUDIO Architecture & Design a été fondé en 2013 par Luka Chaganava et Nino Tchanturia. Notre objectif est de créer des œuvres de haute qualité, intéressantes et originales dans le domaine de l'architecture et du design. Le portefeuille du studio comprend des projets de différents types et échelles, tels que des cliniques, des théâtres, des salles de concert, des hôtels, des centres multifonctionnels et d'affaires, des maisons d'habitation et d'autres projets commerciaux ou privés. Nous nous efforçons d'avoir un impact positif sur l'environnement, l'espace et les personnes, et de contribuer au bon développement de l'architecture et du design.

Notre équipe est composée de professionnels de toutes les spécialités connexes et, nous réalisons des projets d'architecture et de conception complets ; il s'agit de l'une des conditions préalables les plus importantes pour transformer les idées en réalité. Nous pensons qu'il est essentiel de construire notre propre personnalité dans ce domaine, en exprimant le contexte, le contenu, la fonctionnalité et l'individualisme appropriés à chaque travail.

NS STUDIO Architecture & Design fue fundado en 2013 por Luka Chaganava y Nino Tchanturia. Nuestro objetivo es crear obras de alta calidad, interesantes y originales en arquitectura y diseño. La cartera del estudio incluye proyectos de varios tipos y escalas, como clínicas, teatros, salas de conciertos, hoteles, centros multifuncionales y de negocios, casas residenciales y otros proyectos comerciales o privados. A través de ellos nos esforzamos por tener un impacto positivo en el medio ambiente, el espacio y las personas, y por contribuir al correcto desarrollo de la arquitectura y el diseño.

Nuestro equipo está formado por profesionales de todas las especialidades relacionadas, y con su ayuda realizamos proyectos completos de arquitectura y diseño; desde nuestro punto de vista, éste es uno de los requisitos más importantes para convertir las ideas en realidad. Creemos que es vital construir una personalidad propia en este campo, expresando el contexto, el contenido, la funcionalidad y el individualismo adecuados con cada obra; eso hace que nuestro enfoque de los proyectos destaque.

The project area is located in the village of Artana at the foot of the Caucasus mountains. This breathtaking view of the Caucasus became the landmark of a residential house and for a winery. The area is 9 ha in total and a vineyard covers the main part of it. The house and the cellar are located close to the high road. Architectural volumes are decided in the same style, built of old bricks and tiled. The house: our goal was to make the exterior as a part of the interior, so that the volume is towards the main entrance. There was arranged a verdant island in front of the building and a garage next to the house. On the rest of the Northern part of the territory there is vineyard. The single-storey house is built of old bricks and wooden elements, while the roof was tiled. We have created a modern shape with an open courtyard in the center of it and spaces of various function.

La zone du projet est située dans le village d'Artana, au pied des montagnes du Caucase. Cette vue imprenable sur le Caucase est devenue le point de repère d'une maison d'habitation et d'un domaine viticole. La superficie est de 9 ha au total et un vignoble en couvre la majeure partie. La maison et le domaine viticole sont situés près de la route. Les volumes architecturaux ont été décidés dans le même style, construits en briques anciennes et en tuiles. La maison : notre objectif était de faire de l'extérieur une partie de l'intérieur, de sorte que le volume se tourne vers l'entrée principale. Un îlot de verdure a été placé devant le bâtiment et un garage à côté de la maison. Dans le reste de la partie nord du territoire, il y a des vignobles. La maison d'un étage est construite avec de vieilles briques et des éléments en bois, tandis que le toit était fait de tuiles. Nous avons créé une forme moderne avec une cour ouverte au centre et des espaces aux fonctions diverses.

Das Projektgebiet befindet sich im Dorf Artana, am Fuße des Kaukasusgebirges. Dieser atemberaubende Blick auf den Kaukasus wurde zum Wahrzeichen eines Wohnhauses und Weingutes. Die Fläche beträgt insgesamt 9 ha und ein Weinberg bedeckt den größten Teil davon. Das Haus und das Weingut befinden sich in der Nähe der Straße. Die architektonischen Volumina wurden im gleichen Stil beschlossen, mit alten Ziegeln gebaut und gefliest. Das Haus: Unser Ziel war es, das Äußere als Teil des Inneren zu gestalten, so dass sich das Volumen zum Haupteingang hin dreht. Eine Grüninsel wurde vor das Gebäude und eine Garage neben das Haus gesetzt. Im Rest des nördlichen Teils des Territoriums gibt es Weinberge. Das einstöckige Haus ist mit alten Ziegeln und Holzelementen gebaut, während das Dach mit Ziegeln gedeckt wurde. Wir haben eine moderne Form mit einem offenen Innenhof in der Mitte und Räumen mit verschiedenen Funktionen geschaffen.

La zona del proyecto se encuentra en el pueblo de Artana, al pie de las montañas del Cáucaso. Esta impresionante vista del Cáucaso se convirtió en el punto de referencia de una casa residencial y de una bodega. La superficie es de 9 ha en total y un viñedo cubre la mayor parte de ella. La casa y la bodega están situadas cerca de la carretera. Los volúmenes arquitectónicos se decidieron en el mismo estilo, construidos con ladrillos antiguos y alicatados. La casa: nuestro objetivo era hacer el exterior como una parte del interior, de modo que el volumen gira hacia la entrada principal. Se dispuso una isla verde delante del edificio y un garaje junto a la casa. En el resto de la parte norte del territorio hay viñedos. La casa de una sola planta está construida con ladrillos antiguos y elementos de madera, mientras que el tejado era de tejas. Hemos creado una forma moderna con un patio abierto en el centro y espacios de diversa función.

The restaurant "Adre" is located in the historic district, in the center of the old city. It is noteworthy that the restaurant is a part of the complex which also includes a hotel. The constituent elements of the architectural complex are a yard with a two-level terrace and two closed halls of the restaurant connected with it. At the begining stage there were located different types of buildings in the area. During the process of demolition, we came across an old cellar space, dating back to the early 18th century, with all its riches: existing brick walls with arched circles, wooden circular roofing spools and remaining details of the wine vessel Kvevri. Such a discovery encouraged us to restore and preserve all the elements authentically and further emphasize their antiquity and significance through colors. There was arranged a wine hall where special wines of various winemakers are presented.

Le restaurant « Adre » est situé dans le quartier historique, au centre de la vieille ville. Il convient de noter que le restaurant fait partie du complexe qui comprend également un hôtel. Les éléments constitutifs de l'ensemble architectural sont une cour avec une terrasse à deux niveaux et deux salles fermées du restaurant qui y sont reliées. Dans la phase initiale, il y avait différents types de bâtiments dans la zone. Au cours du processus de démolition, nous sommes tombés sur un ancien espace de cave, datant du début du 18e siècle, avec toute sa richesse : murs de briques existants avec des cercles arqués, des bobines de bois pour le toit circulaire et des détails restants de la cuve à vin Kvevri. Cette découverte nous a encouragés à restaurer et à préserver tous les éléments de manière authentique et à mettre davantage en valeur leur ancienneté et leur signification par le biais des couleurs. Une salle des vins a été aménagée dans laquelle sont présentés des vins spéciaux de différents vignerons.

Das Restaurant „Adre" befindet sich im historischen Viertel, im Zentrum der Altstadt. Es ist zu beachten, dass das Restaurant Teil des Komplexes ist, zu dem auch ein Hotel gehört. Die konstituierenden Elemente des architektonischen Komplexes sind ein Hof mit einer zweistöckigen Terrasse und zwei damit verbundene geschlossene Räume des Restaurants. In der Anfangsphase gab es verschiedene Gebäudetypen in dem Gebiet. Bei den Abbrucharbeiten stießen wir auf einen alten Kellerraum vom Anfang des 18. Jahrhunderts mit all seinem Reichtum: bestehende Ziegelmauern mit Rundbögen, Holzspiralen für das runde Dach und verbliebene Details des Kvevri-Weinkessels. Diese Entdeckung ermutigte uns, alle Elemente authentisch zu restaurieren und zu konservieren und ihre Altertümlichkeit und Bedeutung durch Farben noch stärker hervorzuheben. Es wurde ein Weinraum eingerichtet, in dem besondere Weine von verschiedenen Winzern präsentiert werden.

El restaurante "Adre" está situado en el distrito histórico, en el centro de la ciudad vieja. Cabe destacar que el restaurante forma parte del complejo que también incluye un hotel. Los elementos constitutivos del complejo arquitectónico son un patio con una terraza de dos niveles y dos salas cerradas del restaurante conectadas con él. En la fase inicial se encontraban diferentes tipos de edificios en la zona. Durante el proceso de demolición, dimos con un antiguo espacio de bodega, que data de principios del siglo XVIII, con toda su riqueza: paredes de ladrillo existentes con círculos arqueados, bobinas de madera para el tejado circular y detalles restantes de la vasija de vino Kvevri. Este descubrimiento nos animó a restaurar y conservar todos los elementos de forma auténtica y a resaltar aún más su antigüedad y significado a través de los colores. Se dispuso una sala de vinos en la que se presentan vinos especiales de varios bodegueros.

The space that captures you, the place where you lose the sense of time, the atmosphere that makes you calm, it's Vineria, a wine cellar in the central part of Old Tbilisi. From a chaotic, busy street we suddenly get into the space that is completely isolated from the city, street, people, noise, and creates its own world. Prior to the renovation works, there was the abandoned basement with honed walls, remains of old coverings and a lot of useless items. However, the potential of this space was noticeable from the very beginning. Our goal was to create a place, which would make anyone feel comfortable, release from the daily load and get an opportunity of rest.

L'espace qui vous saisit, l'endroit où vous perdez la notion du temps, l'atmosphère qui vous apaise, c'est Vineria, une cave à vin située dans la partie centrale de la vieille ville de Tbilissi. D'une rue chaotique et animée, nous passons soudainement à un espace complètement isolé de la ville, de la rue, des gens, du bruit, et qui crée son propre monde. Avant les travaux de rénovation, le sous-sol était à l'abandon, avec des murs brûlés, des restes d'anciens revêtements et un tas d'objets inutiles. Cependant, le potentiel de cet espace était évident dès le départ. Notre objectif était de créer un lieu où chacun pourrait se sentir à l'aise, se libérer du fardeau quotidien et avoir une chance de se détendre.

Der Raum, der Sie packt, der Ort, an dem Sie die Zeit vergessen, die Atmosphäre, die Sie beruhigt, ist Vineria, ein Weinkeller im zentralen Teil der Altstadt von Tiflis. Von einer chaotischen und belebten Straße geht es plötzlich in einen Raum, der völlig isoliert von der Stadt, von der Straße, von den Menschen, vom Lärm ist und seine eigene Welt schafft. Vor den Renovierungsarbeiten war der Keller verlassen, mit verbrannten Wänden, Resten von alten Verkleidungen und einem Haufen nutzloser Gegenstände. Das Potenzial dieses Raums war jedoch von Anfang an offensichtlich. Unser Ziel war es, einen Ort zu schaffen, an dem sich jeder wohlfühlt, sich von der täglichen Last befreit und die Möglichkeit hat, sich zu entspannen.

El espacio que te atrapa, el lugar en el que pierdes la noción del tiempo, la atmósfera que te tranquiliza, es Vineria, una bodega en la parte central del casco antiguo de Tiflis. De una calle caótica y ajetreada pasamos de repente a un espacio que está completamente aislado de la ciudad, de la calle, de la gente, del ruido, y crea su propio mundo. Antes de las obras de renovación, se encontraba el sótano abandonado con paredes bruñidas, restos de antiguos revestimientos y un montón de objetos inútiles. Sin embargo, el potencial de este espacio se hizo notar desde el principio. Nuestro objetivo era crear un lugar que hiciera que cualquiera se sintiera cómodo, se liberara de la carga diaria y tuviera una oportunidad de descanso.

PLANT
ATELIER PÉTER KIS

WWW.PLANT.CO.HU

> GRAND TOKAJ WINERY
> VILLA PÁTZAY WINE ESTATE

After graduating the Budapest University of Technology and Economics, to start an architectural practice from a small atelier located inside the Budapest Botanical and Zoological Garden in 1997 was a decision which have set the stage for Péter Kis's architecture for the years to come. Besides the various pavilions for animals and visitors scattered around the artificial landscape of the zoo, reconstruction and extension of historic buildings, wineries and further proposals for challenging urban environments characterise the years that followed. An observational attitude, the picturesque, site-specificity, an affinity for re-cultivation and preservation define the practice. Several Hungarian and international awards, recognitions, competition wins, publications and exhibitions attest the quality of the design.

Nach seinem Abschluss an der Budapester Universität für Technik und Wirtschaft war die Gründung eines Architekturbüros aus einer kleinen Werkstatt im Budapester Botanischen und Zoologischen Garten im Jahr 1997 eine Entscheidung, die den Grundstein für Péter Kis' Architektur für die nächsten Jahre legte. Neben den verschiedenen Tier- und Besucherpavillons, die über die künstliche Landschaft des Zoos verstreut sind, prägten der Um- und Ausbau historischer Gebäude, Keller und andere Vorschläge für ein anspruchsvolles städtisches Umfeld die folgenden Jahre. Die beobachtende Haltung, das Pittoreske, die Besonderheit des Ortes und die Affinität zur Wiederverwendung und Erhaltung bestimmen seine Praxis. Mehrere ungarische und internationale Preise, Anerkennungen, Wettbewerbssiege, Publikationen und Ausstellungen zeugen von der Qualität des Designs dieses Studios.

ATELIER PÉTER KIS

Après avoir été diplômé de l'université de technologie et d'économie de Budapest, le lancement d'un cabinet d'architecture dans un petit atelier situé à l'intérieur du jardin botanique et zoologique de Budapest en 1997 a été une décision qui a jeté les bases de l'architecture de Péter Kis pour les années à venir. Outre les divers pavillons pour animaux et visiteurs disséminés dans le paysage artificiel du zoo, la reconstruction et l'extension de bâtiments historiques, de caves et d'autres propositions pour des environnements urbains difficiles ont caractérisé les années suivantes. L'attitude d'observation, le pittoresque, la spécificité du lieu et l'affinité pour la réutilisation et la conservation définissent sa pratique. Plusieurs prix hongrois et internationaux, des reconnaissances, des victoires à des concours, des publications et des expositions attestent de la qualité du design de ce studio.

Tras licenciarse en la Universidad de Tecnología y Economía de Budapest, iniciar un estudio de arquitectura desde un pequeño taller situado en el interior del Jardín Botánico y Zoológico de Budapest en 1997 fue una decisión que ha sentado las bases de la arquitectura de Péter Kis para los años venideros. Además de los diversos pabellones para animales y visitantes repartidos por el paisaje artificial del zoológico, la reconstrucción y ampliación de edificios históricos, bodegas y otras propuestas para entornos urbanos desafiantes caracterizaron los años siguientes. La actitud de observación, lo pintoresco, la especificidad del lugar y la afinidad por la reutilización y la conservación definen su práctica. Varios premios húngaros e internacionales, reconocimientos, victorias en concursos, publicaciones y exposiciones dan fe de la calidad del diseño de este estudio.

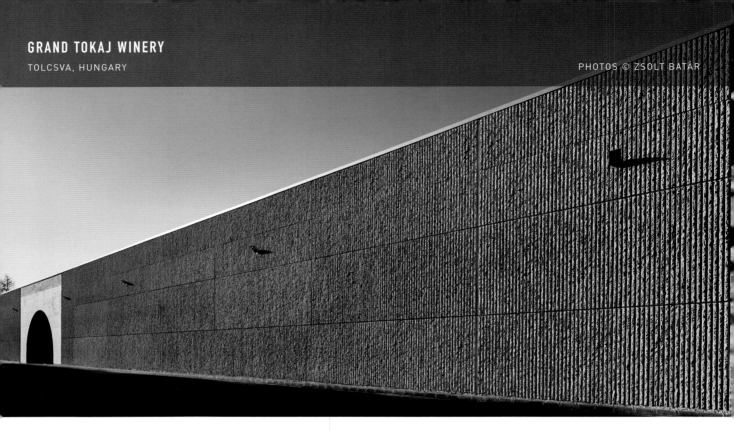

The architectural plan for the winery in the outskirts of Tolcsva displays a multi-layered vision of the slopes of the neighbouring grape fields combined with a scenery of cellars carved in stone, quarries and cave grooves, typical for the region. It's a vision of a winery that is really halfway between a proud industrial building and a modest agricultural cellar. The different elements stand out from the environment without alienation. Parts of the complex are hidden below ground level, while the immediate environment and the tops of the buildings are covered with native vegetation, rubble and detritus, a deliberate symbol of re-cultivation. The mass of the building complex can be perceived visually in different ways: from a distance it gives the impression of a homogeneous rock-like surface, while up close, the fine and detailed plasticity of the façades show up.

Le plan architectural du domaine viticole, situé à la périphérie de Tolcsva, offre une vue à plusieurs niveaux sur les pentes des champs de raisins voisins, combinée à un paysage de caves, de carrières et de grottes sculptées dans la pierre, typiques de la région. Il s'agit d'une vision d'une cave à mi-chemin entre un fier bâtiment industriel et une modeste cave agricole. Les différents éléments se détachent de l'environnement sans s'éloigner les uns des autres. Certaines parties du complexe sont cachées sous le niveau du sol, tandis que les environs immédiats et le sommet des bâtiments sont recouverts de végétation indigène, de débris et de détritus, un symbole délibéré de remise en culture. La masse du complexe immobilier peut être perçue visuellement de différentes manières : de loin, elle donne l'impression d'une surface homogène, semblable à de la roche, tandis que de près, on peut apprécier la plasticité fine et détaillée des façades.

Der architektonische Grundriss des am Ortsrand von Tolcsva gelegenen Weinguts zeigt einen vielschichtigen Blick auf die Hänge der benachbarten Weinfelder, kombiniert mit einer für die Region typischen Kulisse aus in Stein gehauenen Kellern, Steinbrüchen und Höhlengängen. Es ist die Vision eines Weingutes auf halbem Weg zwischen einem stolzen Industriegebäude und einem bescheidenen landwirtschaftlichen Weingut. Die verschiedenen Elemente heben sich von der Umgebung ab, ohne sich gegenseitig zu verfremden. Teile des Komplexes sind unter der Erde verborgen, während die unmittelbare Umgebung und die Dächer der Gebäude mit einheimischer Vegetation, Schutt und Detritus bedeckt sind, ein bewusstes Symbol der Rekultivierung. Die Masse des Gebäudekomplexes kann visuell auf unterschiedliche Weise wahrgenommen werden: Aus der Ferne vermittelt sie den Eindruck einer homogenen, felsenartigen Oberfläche, während aus der Nähe die feine, detaillierte Plastizität der Fassaden zu erkennen ist.

El plan arquitectónico de la bodega, situada en las afueras de Tolcsva, muestra una visión multicapa de las laderas de los campos de uva vecinos, combinada con un escenario de bodegas talladas en piedra, canteras y ranuras de cuevas, típicas de la región. Es una visión de una bodega a medio camino entre un orgulloso edificio industrial y una modesta bodega agrícola. Los distintos elementos destacan del entorno sin alienarse. Algunas partes del complejo están ocultas bajo el nivel del suelo, mientras que el entorno inmediato y la parte superior de los edificios están cubiertos de vegetación autóctona, escombros y detritus, un símbolo deliberado de recultivo. La masa del complejo de edificios puede percibirse visualmente de diferentes maneras: desde la distancia da la impresión de una superficie homogénea parecida a la roca, mientras que de cerca se aprecia la fina y detallada plasticidad de las fachadas.

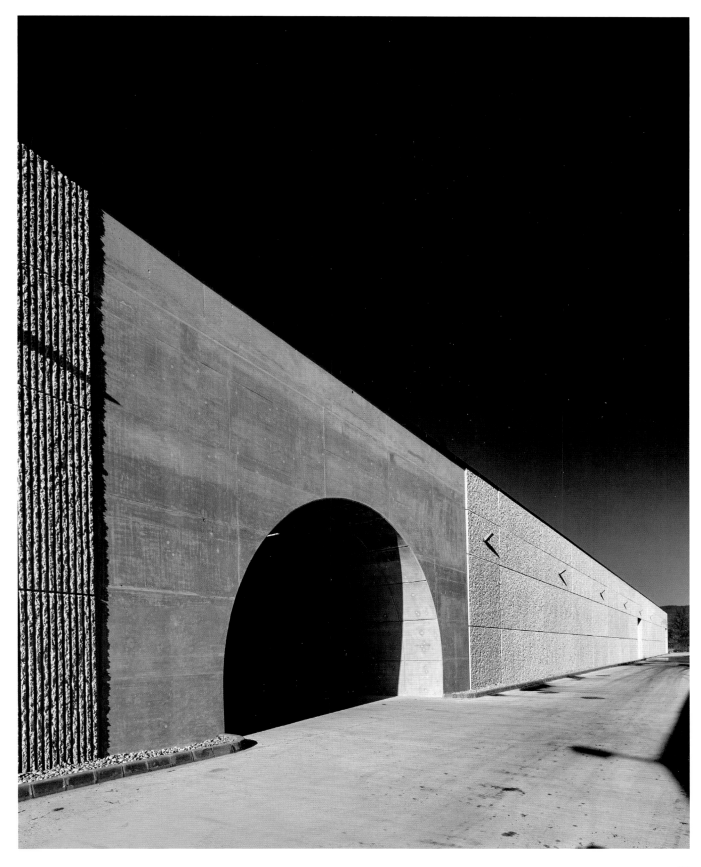

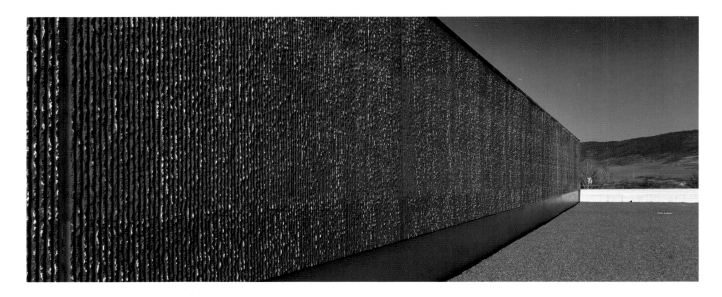

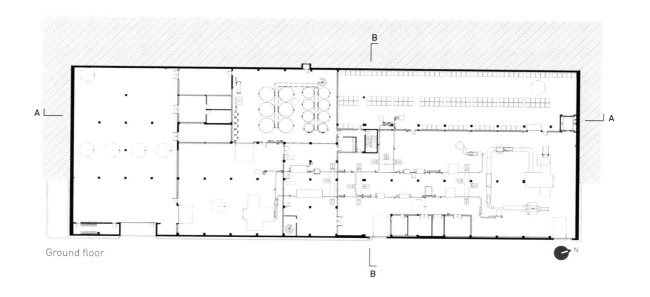

Ground floor

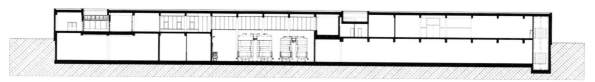

Section A-A

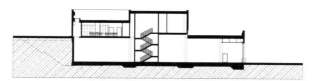

Section B-B

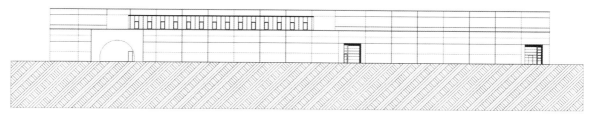

East façade

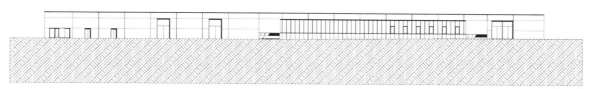

West façade

The processing plant was built in the area of the Balaton Uplands National Park. The plot is stretching long, from the side to the foot of the mountain. The structure was determined by the rational process of winemaking: the chain of the technological spaces is set by the order of the production, both in vertical and horizontal sense. The bending volumes of the building refer to the volcanic activity: emphasizing the proximity of the natural treasures, the basalt pillars and organs characteristic of the region. The archetypical form of the buildings' main façades is reminiscent of the characteristic proportions of the old press houses and the simple, gable-roofed buildings in the neighbourhood. Winding grapevines on the concrete and metal panels lends the uniqueness of the façade.

L'usine de transformation a été construite dans la zone du parc national des hauts plateaux du Balaton. La parcelle s'étend dans le sens de la longueur, du flanc de la colline au pied de la montagne. La structure a été déterminée par le processus rationnel de la vinification : la chaîne des espaces technologiques est fixée par l'ordre de la production, tant verticalement qu'horizontalement. Les volumes courbes du bâtiment font référence à l'activité volcanique : la proximité des trésors naturels, les piliers de basalte et les orgues caractéristiques de la région sont mis en valeur. La forme archétypale des façades principales des bâtiments rappelle les proportions caractéristiques des anciennes maisons de presse et des bâtiments simples à toit à pignon du quartier. Les vignes qui s'enroulent autour des panneaux de béton et de métal confèrent à la façade son caractère unique.

Die Aufbereitungsanlage wurde auf dem Gebiet des Nationalparks Balaton-Oberland gebaut. Das Grundstück erstreckt sich in Längsrichtung, vom Hang bis zum Fuß des Berges. Die Struktur wurde durch den rationalen Prozess der Weinherstellung bestimmt: die Kette der technologischen Räume ist durch die Reihenfolge der Produktion festgelegt, sowohl vertikal als auch horizontal. Die geschwungenen Volumina des Gebäudes verweisen auf die vulkanische Aktivität: Die Nähe zu den Naturschätzen, den Basaltsäulen und den charakteristischen Organen der Region werden betont. Die archetypische Form der Hauptfassaden der Gebäude erinnert an die charakteristischen Proportionen der alten Presshäuser und der einfachen Giebeldachbauten der Nachbarschaft. Die Ranken, die sich um die Beton- und Metallplatten ranken, geben der Fassade ihre Einzigartigkeit.

La planta de procesamiento se construyó en la zona del Parque Nacional de las Tierras Altas del Balatón. La parcela se extiende a lo largo, desde la ladera hasta el pie de la montaña. La estructura fue determinada por el proceso racional de elaboración del vino: la cadena de los espacios tecnológicos está fijada por el orden de la producción, tanto en sentido vertical como horizontal. Los volúmenes curvados del edificio hacen referencia a la actividad volcánica: se destaca la proximidad de los tesoros naturales, los pilares de basalto y los órganos característicos de la región. La forma arquetípica de las fachadas principales de los edificios recuerda las proporciones características de las antiguas casas de la prensa y los sencillos edificios con tejado a dos aguas del barrio. Las vides que se enroscan en los paneles de hormigón y metal confieren la singularidad de la fachada.

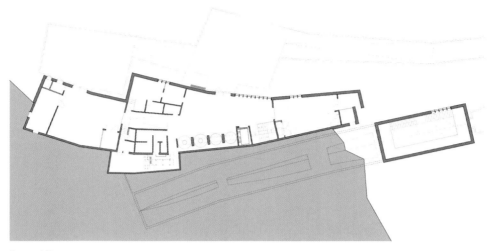

Ground floor

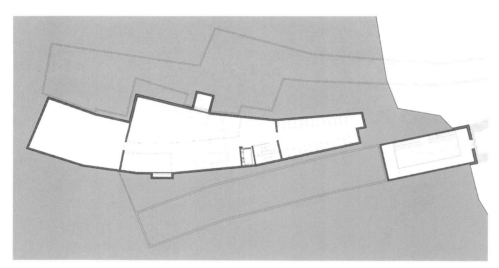

-1 basement level

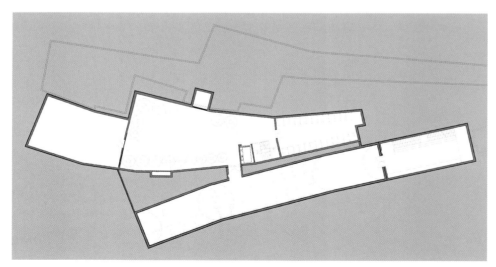

-2 basement level

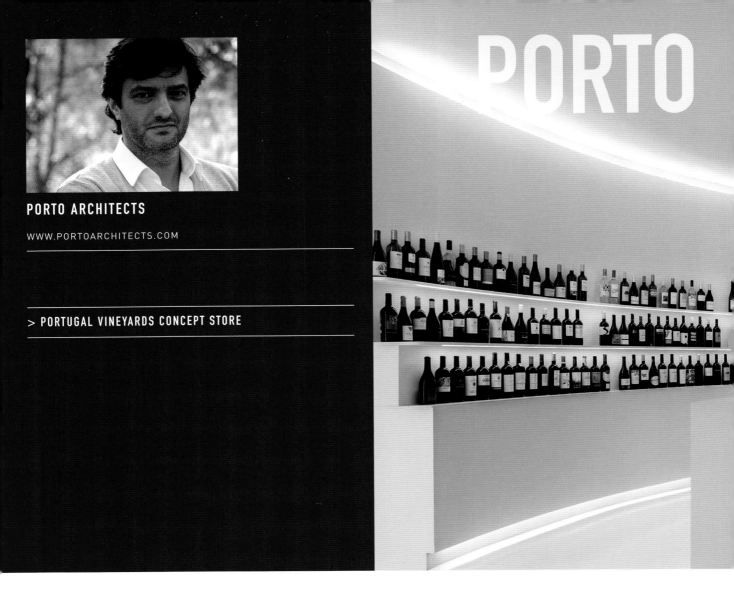

PORTO ARCHITECTS

WWW.PORTOARCHITECTS.COM

> PORTUGAL VINEYARDS CONCEPT STORE

Ricardo Porto Ferreira is a Porto based Portuguese architect who founded Porto Architects in 2019, to build on his design approach that merged from working in big and small-scale projects of previous years. The studio strives to excel in creative design, develop empathy with each individual and have a global network of talent and skills in the design industry that supports the practice capabilities. Ricardo, was a Senior Architect in RMJM Dubai and Turkey, where he designed relevant projects in Istanbul, Jeddah and Dubai. Before moving to the Middle-East he worked for two years in DezOnze, an architectural collaborative studio in Porto. Together with other five architects engaged on a multi-disciplinary practice where the studio opened as an art gallery on the weekends and producing an architectural documentary. With deep roots in architecture and design and 15 years of experience in the industry, he has been considered a retail and hospitality specialist with experience in designing award winning retail destinations and shopping outlets.

Ricardo Porto Ferreira ist ein portugiesischer Architekt mit Sitz in Porto, der 2019 Porto Architects gründete, um auf seinem Designansatz aufzubauen, der sich aus der Arbeit an großen und kleinen Projekten aus den Vorjahren zusammensetzt. Das Studio strebt danach, sich durch kreatives Design auszuzeichnen, Empathie mit jedem Einzelnen zu entwickeln und ein globales Netzwerk von Talenten und Fähigkeiten in der Designbranche zu haben, das die Fähigkeiten des Studios unterstützt. Ricardo, war leitender Architekt bei RMJM Dubai und Türkei, wo er relevante Projekte in Istanbul, Jeddah und Dubai entwarf. Bevor er in den Nahen Osten zog, arbeitete er zwei Jahre lang bei DezOnze, einem kollaborativen Architekturstudio in Porto. Zusammen mit fünf anderen Architekten betrieb er eine multidisziplinäre Praxis, in der das Atelier an Wochenenden als Kunstgalerie geöffnet war und eine Architekturdokumentation produziert wurde. Mit tiefen Wurzeln in Architektur und Design und 15 Jahren Erfahrung in der Branche gilt er als Spezialist für den Einzelhandel und das Gastgewerbe, mit Erfahrung in der Gestaltung von preisgekrönten Einzelhandelszielen und Geschäften.

ARCHITECTS

Ricardo Porto Ferreira est un architecte portugais basé à Porto qui a fondé Porto Architects en 2019, pour s'appuyer sur son approche de conception qui a fusionné en travaillant sur des projets à grande et petite échelle des années précédentes. Le studio s'efforce d'exceller dans la conception créative, de développer l'empathie avec chaque individu et de disposer d'un réseau mondial de talents et de compétences dans le secteur du design.

Ricardo, était architecte principal chez RMJM Dubaï et Turquie, où il a conçu des projets importants à Istanbul, Jeddah et Dubaï. Avant de s'installer au Moyen-Orient, il a travaillé pendant deux ans chez DezOnze, un studio d'architecture collaborative à Porto. Avec cinq autres architectes, il s'est engagé dans une pratique multidisciplinaire dans laquelle l'atelier s'ouvrait comme une galerie d'art le week-end et produisait un documentaire architectural. Avec des racines profondes dans l'architecture et le design et 15 ans d'expérience, il est considéré comme un spécialiste du commerce de détail et de l'hôtellerie, avec une expérience dans la conception de destinations et de magasins de détail primés.

Ricardo Porto Ferreira es un arquitecto portugués afincado en Oporto que fundó Porto Architects en 2019, para aprovechar su enfoque de diseño que se fusionó al trabajar en proyectos de gran y pequeña escala de años anteriores. El estudio se esfuerza por sobresalir en el diseño creativo, desarrollar la empatía con cada individuo y tener una red global de talento y habilidades en la industria del diseño que apoya las capacidades del estudio.

Ricardo, fue arquitecto senior en RMJM Dubai y Turquía, donde diseñó proyectos relevantes en Estambul, Jeddah y Dubai. Antes de trasladarse a Oriente Medio, trabajó durante dos años en DezOnze, un estudio colaborativo de arquitectura en Oporto. Junto con otros cinco arquitectos se dedicó a una práctica multidisciplinar en la que el estudio abría como galería de arte los fines de semana y producía un documental de arquitectura. Con profundas raíces en la arquitectura y el diseño y 15 años de experiencia en el sector, se le considera un especialista en comercio y hostelería, con experiencia en el diseño de destinos comerciales y tiendas premiadas.

The space is blindingly white, minimal and circular. The initial challenges behind the project were to find the answers through geometry, to allow a 600 references display and also a venue for supplier presentations and wine tasting. These requirements were answered through the definition of a radius that allowed the inner circle to create an event for 50 people; a white canvas for the Portuguese wine to shine and be displayed. The shelves are carved out of the walls in reference to the vineyard terraces, in a circular shape that fills the field of view sensitively with indirect lighting and the sharp contrast between the product and the background. This luminance creates the perfect background to observe the diversity the wine represents and a chance to take expression to its core. In this project we planned to celebrate the wine bottle, its shape and the brightness, an interior with a simple form and pure color.

L'espace est d'un blanc aveuglant, minimal et circulaire. Les défis initiaux du projet étaient de trouver les réponses par la géométrie, de permettre une exposition de 600 références et aussi un lieu pour les présentations des fournisseurs et les dégustations de vins. Ces exigences ont été satisfaites en définissant un rayon pour créer un cercle intérieur pour 50 personnes ; une toile blanche pour que le vin portugais brille et soit exposé. Les étagères sont creusées dans les murs en référence aux terrasses des vignobles, dans une forme circulaire qui remplit le champ de vision de manière sensible grâce à l'éclairage indirect et au fort contraste entre le produit et le fond. Cette luminosité crée une toile de fond parfaite pour observer la diversité que représente le vin et une occasion de s'exprimer au cœur de celui-ci. Dans ce projet, nous avons voulu rendre hommage à la bouteille de vin, à sa forme et à sa luminosité, un intérieur aux formes simples et aux couleurs pures.

Der Raum ist blendend weiß, minimal und kreisförmig. Die anfänglichen Herausforderungen des Projekts bestanden darin, die Antworten durch Geometrie zu finden, eine Ausstellung mit 600 Referenzen zu ermöglichen und auch einen Ort für Lieferantenpräsentationen und Weinverkostungen zu schaffen. Diese Anforderungen wurden beantwortet, indem ein Radius definiert wurde, um einen inneren Kreis für 50 Personen zu schaffen; eine weiße Leinwand für portugiesischen Wein, um zu glänzen und sich zu präsentieren. Die Regale sind in Anlehnung an die Terrassen der Weinberge kreisförmig in die Wände eingearbeitet, so dass das Blickfeld durch die indirekte Beleuchtung und den starken Kontrast zwischen Produkt und Hintergrund sensibel ausgefüllt wird. Diese Leuchtkraft schafft die perfekte Kulisse, um die Vielfalt zu beobachten, die der Wein repräsentiert, und eine Gelegenheit, um seinem Kern Ausdruck zu verleihen. In diesem Projekt haben wir uns vorgenommen, der Weinflasche, ihrer Form und ihrem Glanz zu huldigen, ein Interieur mit einer einfachen Form und reiner Farbe.

El espacio es cegadoramente blanco, mínimo y circular. Los retos iniciales del proyecto eran encontrar las respuestas a través de la geometría, para permitir una exposición de 600 referencias y también un lugar para presentaciones de proveedores y catas de vino. Estos requisitos se respondieron mediante la definición de un radio que permitiera crear un círculo interior para 50 personas; un lienzo blanco para que el vino portugués brillara y se expusiera. Las estanterías están talladas en las paredes en referencia a las terrazas de los viñedos, en una forma circular que llena el campo de visión de forma sensible con la iluminación indirecta y el fuerte contraste entre el producto y el fondo. Esta luminosidad crea el fondo perfecto para observar la diversidad que representa el vino y una oportunidad para llevar la expresión a su núcleo. En este proyecto nos planteamos homenajear a la botella de vino, su forma y el brillo, un interior con una forma sencilla y un color puro.

RSAAW | RAFAEL SANTA ANA ARCHITECTURE WORKSHOP

WWW.RSAAW.COM

> COPPER SPIRIT DISTILLERY

Based in Vancouver BC, Canada, RSAAW embodies the multi-dimensional spirit of our beautiful province and cultivates the creation of open, welcome, and safe spaces for all. We are proud of our team's ability to reach a multitude of cultures and are honoured to provide service to a range of peoples and heritages.

Each project undertaken at RSAAW is approached with sustainability and innovation in mind while also commemorating history and culture wherever possible. We are attentive to opportunities to incorporate environmental and social stewardship elements. Our goal in our practice is to seamlessly blend technology and nature into designs that celebrate the diversity of place and people.

Mit Sitz in Vancouver BC, Kanada, verkörpert RSAAW den multidimensionalen Geist unserer schönen Provinz und kultiviert die Schaffung von offenen, einladenden und sicheren Räumen. Wir sind stolz auf die Fähigkeit unseres Teams, eine Vielzahl von Kulturen zu erreichen und fühlen uns geehrt, einer Reihe von Völkern und Herkünften zu dienen.

Jedes Projekt, das bei RSAAW durchgeführt wird, wird mit Blick auf Nachhaltigkeit und Innovation angegangen, während die Geschichte und Kultur, wann immer möglich, in Erinnerung gerufen wird. Wir achten auf Möglichkeiten, Elemente der Umwelt- und Sozialverantwortung zu integrieren. Unser Ziel in unserem Studio ist es, Technologie und Natur nahtlos in Designs zu verbinden, die die Vielfalt von Ort und Menschen feiern.

RSAAW

Basée à Vancouver BC, Canada, RSAAW incarne l'esprit multi-dimensionnel de notre belle province et cultive la création d'espaces ouverts, accueillants et sûrs. Nous sommes fiers de la capacité de notre équipe à toucher une multitude de cultures et nous sommes honorés de servir un éventail de peuples et de patrimoines.

Chaque projet entrepris à RSAAW est abordé dans une optique de durabilité et d'innovation, tout en commémorant l'histoire et la culture dans la mesure du possible. Nous sommes attentifs aux possibilités d'intégrer des éléments de gestion environnementale et sociale. Dans notre studio, notre objectif est de combiner de manière transparente la technologie et la nature dans des conceptions qui célèbrent la diversité des lieux et des personnes.

Con sede en Vancouver BC, Canadá, RSAAW encarna el espíritu multidimensional de nuestra hermosa provincia y cultiva la creación de espacios abiertos, acogedores y seguros. Estamos orgullosos de la capacidad de nuestro equipo para llegar a una multitud de culturas y nos sentimos honrados de prestar servicio a una serie de pueblos y herencias.

Cada proyecto que se lleva a cabo en RSAAW se enfoca teniendo en cuenta la sostenibilidad y la innovación, a la vez que se conmemora la historia y la cultura siempre que sea posible. Estamos atentos a las oportunidades de incorporar elementos de gestión medioambiental y social. Nuestro objetivo en nuestro estudio es combinar a la perfección la tecnología y la naturaleza en diseños que celebren la diversidad del lugar y de las personas.

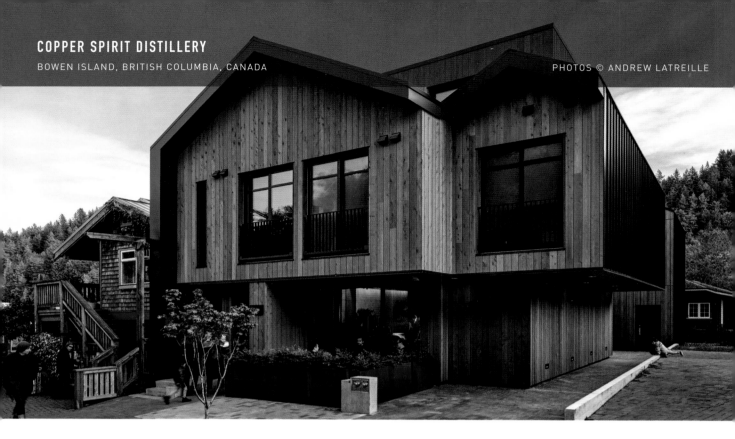

Copper Spirit Distillery is a purpose-built mixed use sustainable building which integrates residential and industrial programs; challenging national code & local urban plan concepts. The building's mass successfully evolved into two separate volumes connected by mechanical systems at basement and by a light-filled atrium above grade that link the public spaces of the building. Visitors experience a minimalist tasting lounge framed by a double height atrium where the 8m. high glazed wall showcases the copper stills and the distilling process. The atrium's glass floor provides a visual connection and allows daylighting into the foundation basement housing the distillery's raw material storage, bottling equipment, and rainwater collection vessels. Focusing on sustainable production, the distillery incorporates rain harvesting and heat recovery systems.

La distillerie Copper Spirit est un bâtiment durable à usage mixte qui intègre des programmes résidentiels et industriels, remettant en question les codes nationaux et les concepts du plan d'urbanisme local. La masse du bâtiment a évolué avec succès en deux volumes distincts reliés par des systèmes mécaniques au sous-sol et par un atrium lumineux au-dessus du sol qui relie les espaces publics du bâtiment. Les visiteurs découvrent une salle de dégustation minimaliste encadrée par un atrium à double hauteur dans lequel un mur vitré de 8 mètres de haut présente les alambics en cuivre et le processus de distillation. Le plancher en verre de l'atrium offre une connexion visuelle et permet à la lumière naturelle de pénétrer dans le sous-sol de la fondation qui abrite le stockage des matières premières de la distillerie, l'équipement d'embouteillage et les cuves de récupération des eaux de pluie. Dans un souci de production durable, la distillerie intègre des systèmes de collecte des eaux de pluie et de récupération de chaleur.

Die Copper Spirit Distillery ist ein nachhaltiges, gemischt genutztes Gebäude, das Wohn- und Industrieprogramme integriert und dabei nationale Vorschriften und lokale Stadtplanungskonzepte herausfordert. Die Masse des Gebäudes hat sich erfolgreich in zwei getrennte Volumen entwickelt, die durch mechanische Systeme im Untergeschoss und durch ein lichtdurchflutetes Atrium im Obergeschoss verbunden sind, das die öffentlichen Räume des Gebäudes verbindet. Der Besucher trifft auf einen minimalistischen Verkostungsraum, der von einem doppelhohen Atrium eingerahmt wird, in dem die 8 m hohe Glaswand die Kupferbrennblasen und den Destillationsprozess zeigt. Der Glasboden des Atriums sorgt für eine visuelle Verbindung und lässt natürliches Licht in das Fundamentuntergeschoss, in dem das Rohmateriallager der Brennerei, die Abfüllanlagen und die Regenwasserauffangbehälter untergebracht sind. Mit dem Fokus auf eine nachhaltige Produktion sind in der Brennerei Systeme zur Regenwassernutzung und Wärmerückgewinnung integriert.

Copper Spirit Distillery es un edificio sostenible de uso mixto que integra programas residenciales e industriales. La masa del edificio ha evolucionado en dos volúmenes separados conectados por sistemas mecánicos en el sótano y por un atrio lleno de luz por encima del nivel que une los espacios públicos del edificio. Los visitantes se encuentran con un salón de degustación enmarcado por un atrio de doble altura en el que la pared acristalada de 8 m. de alto muestra los alambiques de cobre y el proceso de destilación. El suelo de cristal del atrio proporciona una conexión visual y permite la entrada de luz natural en el sótano que alberga el almacenamiento de materias primas, el equipo de embotellado y los recipientes de recogida de agua de lluvia. Centrada en la producción sostenible, la destilería incorpora sistemas de recogida de aguas pluviales y de recuperación de calor.

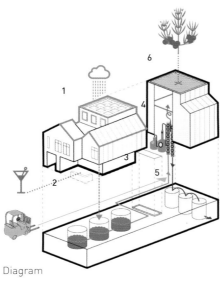

Diagram

1. Water is collected from the North building's roof and then used in the distillation process.
2. Social interaction between the building's users and the public realm.
3. Atrium glass floor brings light into the basement area.
4. Energy produced by the stills to be used as an additional heating source.
5. Grey water control.
6. Roof garden juniper plantings for gin production.

RESIDENCES

Third level

1. Bedroom
2. WC
3. Storage
4. Patio

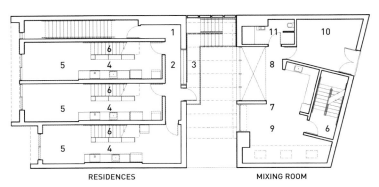

RESIDENCES   **MIXING ROOM**

Second level

1. Residences entry
2. Corridor
3. Emergency exit / balcony
4. Kitchen
5. Living
6. Stairs
7. Mixing room
8. Viewing corridor
9. Bottling + storage
10. Office
11. WC

TASTING LOUNGE   **DISTILLERY ROOM**

Ground level

1. Entry
2. Tasting lounge
3. Kitchen
4. Patio
5. WC
6. Storage
7. Atrium
8. Corridor
9. Distillery
10. Recycling
11. Stairs
12. Residence entry

CELLAR

Basement level

1. Rain water collection chamber
2. Grain storage
3. Aging barrels
4. Water treatment shaft
5. Mechanical
6. Eelctrical

0   3m   N

SEVERIN PROEKT

WWW.SEVERINPROEKT.RU

> COTE ROCHEUSE WINERY

Founded in 1993 by architect Alexander Balabin, SEVERIN PROEKT is one of the leading architectural companies in Russia. We work for buildings for various purposes, from public facilities to residential and industrial complexes.

We design all stages, including the concept and detailed documentation based on our advanced expertise in building informational modelling.

We believe in the paramount role of rationalism in the creative process; the groundwork for efficient and inspiring architecture for buildings of any purpose. We consider how people will move, feel, evolve and settle in and about our buildings.

Alexander Balabin is an expert speaker and lecturer. A selection of his architectural graphics was displayed at Schusev State Museum of Architecture and stays in museum collection. He is a member of the Union of Architects of Russia, professor at the International Academy of Architecture, Moscow Campus.

SEVERIN PROEKT wurde 1993 vom Architekten Alexander Balabin gegründet und ist eines der führenden Architekturbüros in Russland. Wir arbeiten an Gebäuden verschiedenster Art, von öffentlichen Einrichtungen bis hin zu Wohn- und Industriekomplexen.

Wir planen alle Phasen, einschließlich Konzept und detaillierter Dokumentation, basierend auf unserer fortgeschrittenen Expertise in der Modellierung von Gebäudeinformationen.

Wir glauben an die primäre Rolle des Rationalismus im kreativen Prozess; die Basis für effiziente und inspirierende Architektur für Gebäude jeglicher Art. Wir berücksichtigen, wie sich Menschen in unseren Gebäuden bewegen, fühlen, entwickeln und niederlassen werden.

Alexander Balabin ist Fachreferent und Dozent. Eine Auswahl seiner architektonischen Grafiken wurde im Schusev State Museum of Architecture ausgestellt und verbleibt in der Sammlung des Museums. Er ist Mitglied der Union der Architekten Russlands und Professor an der Internationalen Akademie für Architektur, Abteilung Moskau.

SEVERIN PROEKT

Fondé en 1993 par l'architecte Alexander Balabin, SEVERIN PROEKT est l'un des principaux cabinets d'architectes en Russie. Nous travaillons sur des bâtiments de différents types, des installations publiques aux complexes résidentiels et industriels. Nous concevons toutes les étapes, y compris le concept et la documentation détaillée, sur la base de notre expertise avancée en matière de modélisation informationnelle des bâtiments.

Nous croyons au rôle primordial du rationalisme dans le processus de création, base d'une architecture efficace et inspirante pour les bâtiments de toute nature. Nous tenons compte de la manière dont les gens vont se déplacer, se sentir, évoluer et s'installer dans nos bâtiments.

Alexander Balabin est un orateur expert et un conférencier. Une sélection de ses graphiques architecturaux a été exposée au Musée d'architecture d'État Schusev et fait partie de la collection du musée. Il est membre de l'Union des architectes de Russie et professeur à l'Académie internationale d'architecture, branche de Moscou.

Fundada en 1993 por el arquitecto Alexander Balabin, SEVERIN PROEKT es una de las principales empresas de arquitectura de Rusia. Trabajamos en edificios de diversa índole, desde instalaciones públicas hasta complejos residenciales e industriales. Diseñamos todas las etapas, incluyendo el concepto y la documentación detallada, basándonos en nuestra avanzada experiencia en la modelización informática de edificios.

Creemos en el papel primordial del racionalismo en el proceso creativo; la base para una arquitectura eficiente e inspiradora para edificios de cualquier propósito. Tenemos en cuenta cómo las personas se moverán, sentirán, evolucionarán y se instalarán en nuestros edificios.

Alexander Balabin es un experto orador y conferenciante. Una selección de sus gráficos arquitectónicos se expuso en el Museo Estatal de Arquitectura Schusev y permanece en la colección del museo. Es miembro de la Unión de Arquitectos de Rusia y profesor de la Academia Internacional de Arquitectura, sede de Moscú.

COTE ROCHEUSE WINERY

VARVAROVKA VILLAGE, ANAPA, KRASNODAR REGION, RUSSIA

A beautiful vineyard was planted right on the Black Sea coast. Wine production in Cote Rocheuse is based on the principles of gravitational winemaking which drives the winery architectural plan. The whole technology that needs a significant height enclosed in a simple rectangular volume, that is integrated into the slope on the site. The production spaces are placed on different levels so the juice travels by gravity from the first tanks to those in the cellar. The upper "capsule" is focused on the public areas. The roof has access for those who want to catch a spectacular view. The perception of the winery is determined by the antithesis "rectangular vs. bionic" or "technocratic vs natural". The building looks completely different from various angles and depending on the light the concrete shell looks either almost snow-white or dark gray. It is also designed for the perception from a bird's-eye view as a helipad is equipped in the neighborhood.

Un magnifique vignoble a été planté sur la côte de la mer Noire. La production de vin à Cote Rocheuse est basée sur les principes de la viticulture gravitationnelle qui détermine le plan architectural de la cave. Toute la technologie qui nécessite une hauteur importante est enfermée dans un simple volume rectangulaire, qui s'intègre dans la pente du terrain. Les espaces de production sont placés sur différents niveaux afin que le jus voyage par gravité des premières cuves aux cuves de la cave. La « capsule » supérieure se concentre sur les espaces publics. La terrasse du toit est accessible pour ceux qui veulent profiter d'une vue spectaculaire. La perception de la cave est déterminée par l'antithèse « rectangulaire vs. bionique » ou « technocratique vs. naturel ». Le bâtiment a un aspect complètement différent selon l'angle sous lequel on le regarde et, selon la lumière, la coque en béton apparaît presque blanche ou gris foncé. Il est également conçu pour une vue à vol d'oiseau puisqu'il est équipé d'un héliport dans le quartier où il se trouve.

Direkt an der Schwarzmeerküste wurde ein schöner Weinberg angelegt. Die Weinproduktion an der Cote Rocheuse basiert auf den Prinzipien des Gravitationsweinbaus, der den architektonischen Plan des Weinguts bestimmt. Die gesamte Technik, die eine nennenswerte Höhe benötigt, ist in einem einfachen rechteckigen Volumen untergebracht, das in den Hang des Grundstücks integriert ist. Die Produktionsräume sind auf verschiedenen Ebenen angeordnet, so dass der Saft durch die Schwerkraft von den ersten Tanks zu den Kellertanks wandert. Die obere „Kapsel" konzentriert sich auf die öffentlichen Bereiche. Die Dachterrasse hat Zugang für diejenigen, die eine spektakuläre Aussicht genießen wollen. Die Wahrnehmung des Weingutes wird durch die Antithese „rechteckig vs. bionisch" oder „technokratisch vs. natürlich" bestimmt. Das Gebäude sieht aus verschiedenen Blickwinkeln völlig unterschiedlich aus und je nach Lichteinfall erscheint die Betonhülle fast weiß oder dunkelgrau. Es ist auch für die Vogelperspektive konzipiert, da es mit einem Hubschrauberlandeplatz in der Nachbarschaft ausgestattet ist, wo es sich befindet.

El viñedo fue plantado en la costa del Mar Negro. La producción de vino en Cote Rocheuse se basa en los principios de la viticultura gravitacional. La tecnología que necesita más altura se encierra en un volumen rectangular, integrado en la pendiente del terreno. Los espacios de producción se sitúan en diferentes niveles, así el zumo viaja por gravedad desde los primeros depósitos hasta los de la bodega. La "cápsula" superior se centra en las zonas públicas. La azotea tiene acceso para los que quieran disfrutar de una vista espectacular. La percepción de la bodega está determinada por la antítesis "rectangular vs. biónica" o "tecnocrática vs. natural". El edificio tiene un aspecto completamente diferente desde varios ángulos y, dependiendo de la luz, el armazón de hormigón parece casi blanco o de color gris oscuro. También está diseñado para la percepción a vista de pájaro ya que está equipado con un helipuerto en el barrio en el que se encuentra.

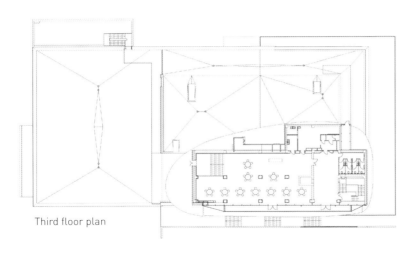

Third floor plan

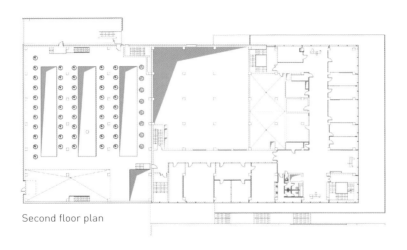

Second floor plan

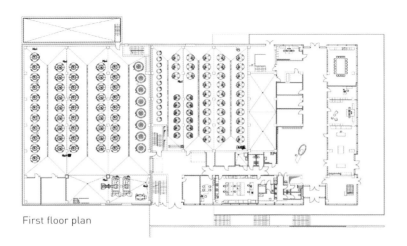

First floor plan

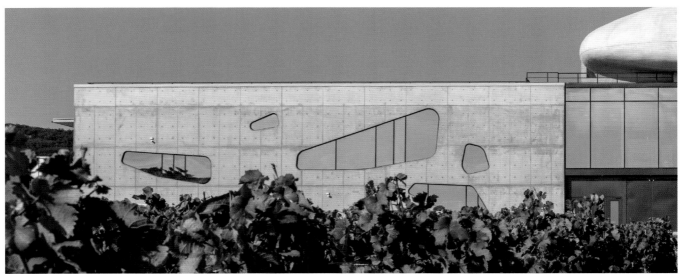

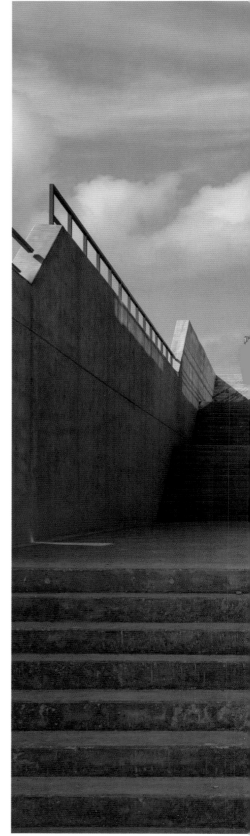

225

SRTA. ROTTENMEIER

WWW.SRTAROTTENMEIER.COM

> BODEGA CASA ROJO
> BODEGA VIRGEN DE LAS VIÑAS

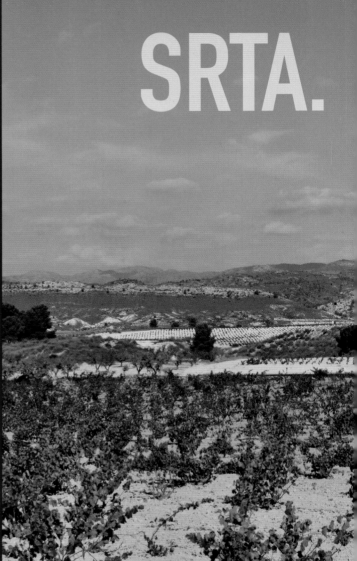

SRTA.

Perfection. That is Srta. Rottenmeier's maxim. Young, fresh, dreamers, these are the members of this team of architects who are always looking for their work to prevail over time and cross borders.

José Manuel and Gemma, directors of the studio, are dreamers who create life in every project they manage. The use of noble materials, the integration of natural light and respect for the environment define the Mediterranean architecture of their buildings. It is a true symbiosis between beauty and functionality, generating a dialogue between those who live in it and those who design it, creating spaces that transmit harmony, peace and well-being.

Vollkommenheit. Das ist die Maxime von Srta. Rottenmeier. Jung, frisch, träumerisch, das sind die Mitglieder dieses Architektenteams, die immer darauf bedacht sind, dass sich ihre Arbeit im Laufe der Zeit durchsetzt und Grenzen überschreitet.

José Manuel und Gemma, die Leiter des Studios, sind Träumer, die in jedem Werk, das sie inszenieren, Leben schaffen. Die Verwendung edler Materialien, die Integration von natürlichem Licht und der Respekt vor der Umwelt bestimmen die mediterrane Architektur ihrer Gebäude. Es ist eine echte Symbiose zwischen Schönheit und Funktionalität, die einen Dialog zwischen den Bewohnern und den Gestaltern erzeugt und Räume schafft, die Harmonie, Ruhe und Wohlbefinden vermitteln.

ROTTENMEIER

La perfection. C'est la maxime de Srta. Rottenmeier. Jeunes, frais, rêveurs, tels sont les membres de cette équipe d'architectes qui cherchent toujours à ce que leur travail prévale sur le temps et traverse les frontières.

José Manuel et Gemma, directeurs du studio, sont des rêveurs qui créent la vie dans chaque œuvre qu'ils réalisent. L'utilisation de matériaux nobles, l'intégration de la lumière naturelle et le respect de l'environnement définissent l'architecture méditerranéenne de leurs bâtiments. Il s'agit d'une véritable symbiose entre beauté et fonctionnalité, générant un dialogue entre ceux qui l'habitent et ceux qui le conçoivent, créant des espaces qui transmettent harmonie, paix et bien-être.

La perfección. Esa es la máxima de Srta. Rottenmeier. Jóvenes, frescos, soñadores, así son los integrantes de este equipo de arquitectos que buscan siempre que sus trabajos prevalezcan en el tiempo y que traspasen fronteras.

José Manuel y Gemma, directores del estudio, son unos soñadores que crean vida en cada obra que dirigen. El uso de materiales nobles, la integración de la luz natural y el respeto por el entorno, definen la arquitectura mediterránea de sus edificios. Se trata de una verdadera simbiosis entre belleza y funcionalidad, generando un diálogo entre quien lo habita y quien lo diseña, creando espacios que transmiten armonía, paz y bienestar.

This winery was not only designed to make wine, but as a space to share and enjoy an oenological experience. The place is the main protagonist of the project where nature and silence transmit a deep sense of peace. The interior space is visually connected to the natural environment through large openings that frame the landscape. The use of traditional materials such as white stucco, ceramics and wood connect the building with the materials used in the ageing of wine over the years.

The building integrates the industrial and social areas, with no apparent distinction from the outside. The southern area houses the offices, tasting area and wine tourism visits, while the northern part and the basement are reserved for winemaking, rooms that need to be protected from the heat and solar radiation.

Cette cave n'a pas été conçue uniquement pour produire du vin, mais aussi comme un espace pour partager et apprécier une expérience œnologique. Le lieu est le principal protagoniste du projet, où la nature et le silence transmettent un profond sentiment de paix. L'espace intérieur est visuellement relié à l'environnement naturel par de grandes ouvertures qui encadrent le paysage. L'utilisation de matériaux traditionnels tels que le stuc blanc, la céramique et le bois relie le bâtiment aux matériaux utilisés pour le vieillissement du vin au fil des ans.

Le bâtiment intègre les zones industrielles et sociales, sans distinction apparente depuis l'extérieur. Dans la zone sud se trouvent les bureaux, l'espace de dégustation et les visites œnotouristiques ; la partie nord et le sous-sol sont réservés à la vinification, des pièces qui doivent être protégées de la chaleur et du rayonnement solaire.

Dieses Weingut wurde nicht nur entworfen, um Wein zu machen, sondern als ein Raum, um eine önologische Erfahrung zu teilen und zu genießen. Der Ort ist der Hauptprotagonist des Projekts, wo die Natur und die Stille ein tiefes Gefühl des Friedens vermitteln. Der Innenraum ist durch große Öffnungen, die die Landschaft einrahmen, visuell mit der natürlichen Umgebung verbunden. Die Verwendung traditioneller Materialien wie weißer Stuck, Keramik und Holz verbinden das Gebäude mit den Materialien, die im Laufe der Jahre für die Reifung von Wein verwendet wurden.

Das Gebäude integriert den Industrie- und Sozialbereich, ohne dass von außen ein Unterschied erkennbar ist. Im südlichen Bereich befinden sich die Büros, der Verkostungsbereich und die Weintourismusbesuche; der nördliche Teil und das Untergeschoss sind für die Weinherstellung reserviert, Räume, die vor Hitze und Sonneneinstrahlung geschützt werden müssen.

Esta bodega no sólo fue diseñada para hacer vino, sino como un espacio para compartir y disfrutar de una experiencia enológica. El lugar es el principal protagonista del proyecto donde la naturaleza y el silencio transmiten una profunda sensación de paz. El espacio interior queda conectado visualmente con el medio natural a través de grandes huecos que enmarcan el paisaje. La utilización de materiales tradicionales como el estuco blanco, la cerámica y la madera conectan al edificio con los materiales utilizados en la crianza del vino a lo largo de los años.

El edificio integra la zona industrial y social, sin una distinción aparente desde el exterior. En la zona sur se sitúan las oficinas, zona de catas y visitas de enoturismo; reservando la parte norte y el subsuelo para la elaboración del vino, estancias que necesitan estar protegidas del calor y la radiación solar.

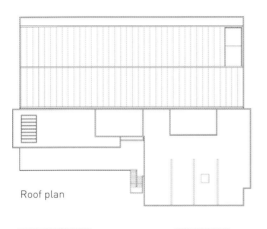

Roof plan

First floor plan

1. Viewing terrace
2. Living-dining room
3. Kitchen
4. Toilets
5. Workers' areas
6. Telecommunications room
7. Meeting room
8. Deputy director's office
9. Director's office
10. Boardroom
11. Mezzanine
12. Machine terrace

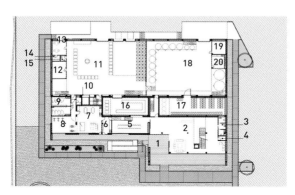

Floor plan

1. Entrance
2. Reception
3. Toilets
4. Archive
5. Tasting room
6. Office
7. Staff room
8. Gymnasium
9. Changing rooms
10. Cleaning room
11. Dispatch
12. Parcel
13. Logistics
14. Archive
15. Toilet
16. Labelling
17. Barrel room
18. Processing plant
19. Warehouse
20. Laboratory

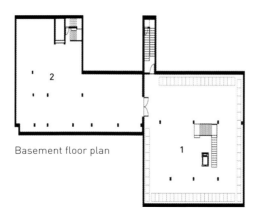

Basement floor plan

1. Bottle room
2. Storage room

BODEGA VIRGEN DE LAS VIÑAS

TOMELLOSO, CIUDAD REAL, SPAIN

At a depth of 7 m dug into the ground, hundreds of passages and production tanks were abandoned for more than 30 years when the industry and wine production of this winery was modernised.
Srta. Rottenmeier has designed the rehabilitation and adaptation project for the musealisation of the complex, where the main intervention has been to rescue the original walls that were in contact with the wine for so long and where the marks are still visible, to convert the space into an imposing, cold, sober and dark exhibition container where the history of the place can be perceived, reserving the light beam for the tools and implements exhibited, which will focus the attention of the exhibition element.

A une profondeur de 7 m creusée dans le sol, des centaines de passages et de cuves de production ont été abandonnés pendant plus de 30 ans lors de la modernisation de l'industrie et de la production de vin de cette cave.
Srta. Rottenmeier a conçu le projet de réhabilitation et d'adaptation pour la muséalisation du complexe, où l'intervention principale a été de sauver les murs originaux qui ont été en contact avec le vin pendant si longtemps et où les marques sont encore visibles, pour convertir l'espace en un conteneur d'exposition imposant, froid, sobre et sombre où l'histoire du lieu est perçue, réservant aux outils et aux instruments exposés, le faisceau de lumière qui focalisera l'attention de l'élément d'exposition.

In einer Tiefe von 7 m in den Boden gegraben, wurden Hunderte von Gängen und Produktionstanks für mehr als 30 Jahre aufgegeben, als die Industrie und die Weinproduktion dieser Weinkellerei modernisiert wurde.
Srta. Rottenmeier hat das Sanierungs- und Anpassungsprojekt für die Musealisierung des Komplexes entworfen, bei dem der Haupteingriff darin bestand, die ursprünglichen Wände zu retten, die so lange mit dem Wein in Berührung waren und an denen die Spuren noch sichtbar sind, den Raum in einen imposanten, kalten, nüchternen und dunklen Ausstellungscontainer umzuwandeln, in dem die Geschichte des Ortes wahrgenommen wird, wobei den ausgestellten Werkzeugen und Geräten der Lichtstrahl vorbehalten bleibt, der die Aufmerksamkeit des Ausstellungselements fokussiert.

A 7 m de profundidad excavados sobre el terreno, cientos de pasadizos y depósitos de elaboración quedaron abandonados durante más de 30 años al modernizarse la industria y producción de vino de esta bodega.
Srta. Rottenmeier ha diseñado el proyecto de rehabilitación y adaptación para la musealización del conjunto, donde la principal intervención ha sido rescatar los muros originales que tanto tiempo estuvieron en contacto con el vino y donde aún se dejan entrever las marcas, para convertir el espacio en un contendor expositivo imponente, frío, sobrio y tenebroso donde se perciba la historial del lugar, reservando para las herramientas y aperos exhibidos, el haz de luz que hará que se focalice la atención del elemento expositivo.

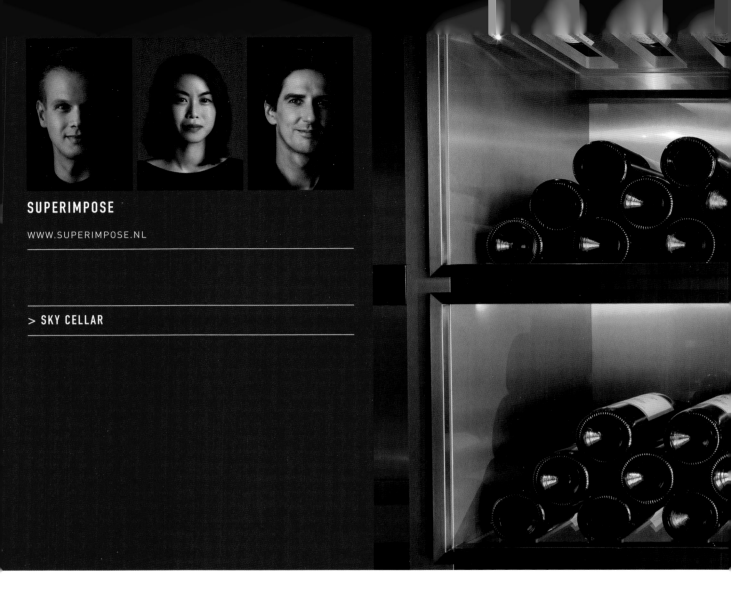

SUPERIMPOSE

WWW.SUPERIMPOSE.NL

> SKY CELLAR

Superimpose is a creativity driven studio. The founders continuously envision, challenge, focus, and elevate concepts throughout each phase of each design project to foster bold and striking visions. We strongly believe in designing with contextual awareness and applying problem solving tactics. Our work is based on the most valid contextual components and overlay them with carefully considered architecture elements. We design with the responsibility to improve, protect, recycle and sustain both our natural and built environments. Our designs enrich the context by giving back a design that adds value, aesthetic and identity to the place. We believe design is not a sole commodity and value all forms off collaboration, and appreciate all client input and possible inspiration. Our design scope covers from architecture to masterplan projects, interior and installation design. We also highly value local initiatives such as Micr-O project in Hangzhou.

Superimpose ist ein von Kreativität getriebenes Studio. Die Gründer stellen sich kontinuierlich vor, fordern heraus, fokussieren und erhöhen die Konzepte in jeder Phase eines jeden Designprojekts, um kühne und wirkungsvolle Visionen zu fördern. Wir glauben fest an kontextbewusstes Design und die Anwendung von Problemlösungstaktiken. Unsere Arbeit basiert auf den gültigsten kontextuellen Komponenten und wir überlagern sie mit sorgfältig durchdachten Architekturelementen. Wir entwerfen mit der Verantwortung, sowohl unsere natürliche als auch unsere gebaute Umwelt zu verbessern, zu schützen, zu recyceln und zu erhalten. Unsere Entwürfe bereichern den Kontext, indem sie ein Design liefern, das dem Ort Wert, Ästhetik und Identität verleiht. Wir glauben, dass Design kein einzelnes Produkt ist, und schätzen alle Formen der Zusammenarbeit. Wir schätzen jeden Kundeninput und jede potenzielle Inspiration. Unser Gestaltungsspektrum reicht von der Architektur über Masterplanprojekte bis hin zu Innenarchitektur und Installationen. Wir schätzen auch lokale Initiativen sehr, wie das Micr-O-Projekt in Hangzhou.

SUPERIMPOSE

Superimpose est un studio animé par la créativité. Les fondateurs ne cessent d'imaginer, de mettre au défi, de cibler et d'élever les concepts à chaque phase de chaque projet de conception afin de favoriser des visions audacieuses et percutantes. Nous croyons fermement à la conception contextuelle et à l'application de tactiques de résolution de problèmes. Notre travail est basé sur les composantes contextuelles les plus valables et nous les superposons à des éléments architecturaux soigneusement étudiés. Nous concevons avec la responsabilité d'améliorer, de protéger, de recycler et de soutenir nos environnements naturels et bâtis. Nos conceptions enrichissent le contexte en renvoyant un design qui ajoute de la valeur, de l'esthétique et de l'identité au lieu. Nous apprécions toutes les formes de collaboration, ainsi que toutes les contributions et inspirations potentielles des clients. Notre champ d'action s'étend de l'architecture aux projets de plans directeurs, en passant par l'aménagement intérieur et les installations. Nous accordons également une grande importance aux initiatives locales, telles que le projet Micr-O à Hangzhou.

Superimpose es un estudio impulsado por la creatividad. Los fundadores continuamente imaginan, desafían, enfocan y elevan los conceptos a través de cada fase de cada proyecto de diseño para fomentar visiones audaces e impactantes. Creemos firmemente en el diseño con conciencia contextual y en la aplicación de tácticas de resolución de problemas. Nuestro trabajo se basa en los componentes contextuales más válidos y los superponemos con elementos de arquitectura cuidadosamente considerados. Diseñamos con la responsabilidad de mejorar, proteger, reciclar y sostener tanto nuestro entorno natural como el construido. Nuestros diseños enriquecen el contexto devolviendo un diseño que añade valor, estética e identidad al lugar. Creemos que el diseño no es un producto único y valoramos todas las formas de colaboración, y apreciamos todas las aportaciones del cliente y su posible inspiración. Nuestro ámbito de diseño abarca desde la arquitectura hasta los proyectos de planes maestros, pasando por el diseño de interiores e instalaciones. También valoramos mucho las iniciativas locales, como el proyecto Micr-O en Hangzhou.

The project is situated at the top floor of one of Beijing's newest and most high-end tower developments, the Genesis Community. Genesis Beijing is a mixed-use development combining a hotel, offices, gardens and a museum by Japanese Architect Tadao Ando. The club's members will only be accessible to a private and selected group. There is where the client organizes gatherings and stores and consumes his valuable wine and tea collection. The space is divided by a central element creating two distinctive worlds: the client's office space and the private member's club. Members enter through a hidden pivot-door into the exclusive member's club that instantly offers spectacular views over Beijing's embassy and financial districts. The golden stainless steel central element subtly reflects the skyline and naturally forms a backdrop of the entire club.

Le projet est situé au dernier étage de l'une des tours les plus récentes et les plus haut de gamme de Pékin, la Genesis Community. Genesis Beijing est un projet à usage mixte combinant un hôtel, des bureaux, des jardins et un musée, conçu par l'architecte japonais Tadao Ando. Seul un groupe restreint et privé aura accès aux membres du club. C'est ici que le client organise ses réunions et stocke et consomme sa précieuse collection de vins et de thés. L'espace est divisé par un élément central qui crée deux mondes distincts : les bureaux du client et le club privé des membres. Les membres entrent par une porte pivotante dissimulée dans le club exclusif qui offre instantanément une vue spectaculaire sur les quartiers des ambassades et des finances de Pékin. L'élément central en acier inoxydable doré reflète subtilement la ligne d'horizon et constitue naturellement la toile de fond de l'ensemble de l'espace.

Das Projekt befindet sich in der obersten Etage eines der neuesten und hochwertigsten Türme Pekings, der Genesis Community. Genesis Beijing ist ein gemischt genutztes Projekt, das ein Hotel, Büros, Gärten und ein Museum des japanischen Architekten Tadao Ando kombiniert. Nur ein ausgewählter, privater Kreis hat Zugang zu den Clubmitgliedern. Hier organisiert der Kunde Meetings und lagert und konsumiert seine wertvolle Wein- und Teesammlung. Der Raum wird durch ein zentrales Element geteilt, das zwei unterschiedliche Welten schafft: die Büroräume des Kunden und den privaten Mitgliederclub. Die Mitglieder betreten den exklusiven Club durch eine verborgene Drehtür, die sofort einen spektakulären Blick auf das Botschafts- und Finanzviertel von Peking bietet. Das zentrale goldene Edelstahlelement reflektiert subtil die Skyline und bildet natürlich den Hintergrund für den gesamten Raum.

El proyecto está situado en la última planta de una de las torres más nuevas y de más alto nivel de Pekín, la Comunidad Génesis. Genesis Beijing es un desarrollo de uso mixto que combina un hotel, oficinas, jardines y un museo del arquitecto japonés Tadao Ando. A los miembros del club sólo podrá acceder un grupo privado y selecto. Allí es donde el cliente organiza reuniones y almacena y consume su valiosa colección de vino y té. El espacio está dividido por un elemento central que crea dos mundos distintos: el espacio de la oficina del cliente y el club privado de socios. Los miembros entran a través de una puerta pivotante oculta en el exclusivo club que ofrece al instante unas vistas espectaculares sobre la embajada y los distritos financieros de Pekín. El elemento central de acero inoxidable dorado refleja sutilmente la línea del horizonte y constituye naturalmente el telón de fondo de todo el espacio.

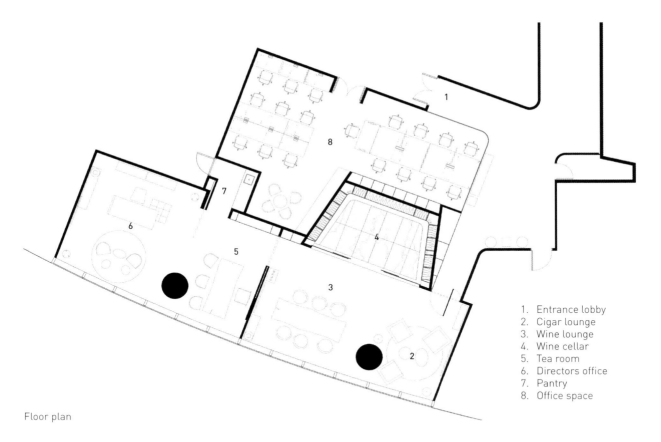

Floor plan

1. Entrance lobby
2. Cigar lounge
3. Wine lounge
4. Wine cellar
5. Tea room
6. Directors office
7. Pantry
8. Office space

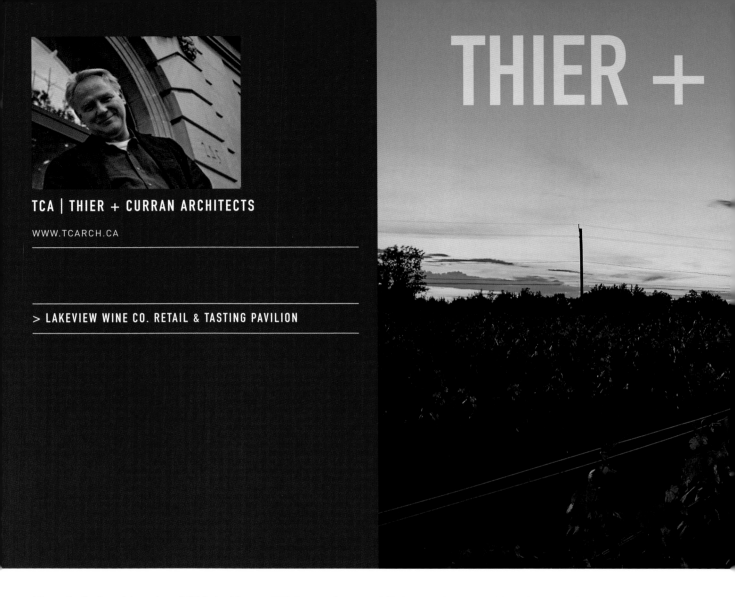

TCA | THIER + CURRAN ARCHITECTS

WWW.TCARCH.CA

> LAKEVIEW WINE CO. RETAIL & TASTING PAVILION

THIER +

The principal and founder of TCA Architects, Bill Curran is an accomplished designer. Bill's hands-on and pro-active approach ensures that design goals and quality standards are maintained for all the firm's work.

Bill's keen design sense guides all of TCA's projects. His ability to astutely observe, communicate, and, most importantly, listen, has allowed him to successfully collaborate with clients to exceed their goals with innovative designs that transcend the ordinary.

His bold use of colour, attention to design details, and dedication to craft, result in projects that are decidedly modern, while still warm and inviting. His use of natural materials such as wood and stone lends tactility to TCA's designs, along with his focus on the quality of the user experience ensures that TCA's buildings are places where people feel welcomed and comfortable.

Bill Curran, Leiter und Gründer von TCA Architects, ist ein versierter Designer. Sein praktischer und proaktiver Ansatz stellt sicher, dass die Designziele und Qualitätsstandards während der gesamten Arbeit der Firma eingehalten werden.

Bills ausgeprägter Sinn für Design leitet alle Projekte von TCA. Seine Fähigkeit, zu beobachten, zu kommunizieren und vor allem zuzuhören, hat es ihm ermöglicht, erfolgreich mit Kunden zusammenzuarbeiten, um deren Ziele mit innovativen Designs zu übertreffen, die über das Gewöhnliche hinausgehen.

Ihre kühne Verwendung von Farben, ihre Aufmerksamkeit für Designdetails und ihre Hingabe an die Handwerkskunst resultieren in Projekten, die entschieden modern, aber dennoch warm und einladend sind. Die Verwendung natürlicher Materialien wie Holz und Stein verleiht den Entwürfen von TCA ein taktiles Gefühl, und ihre Aufmerksamkeit für das Nutzererlebnis stellt sicher, dass TCA-Gebäude Orte sind, an denen sich Menschen willkommen und wohl fühlen.

CURRAN ARCHITECTS

Bill Curran, principal et fondateur de TCA Architects, est un designer accompli. Son approche pratique et proactive garantit le maintien des objectifs de conception et des normes de qualité tout au long du travail de l'entreprise.

Le sens aigu du design de Bill guide tous les projets de TCA. Sa capacité d'observation, de communication et, surtout, d'écoute, lui a permis de collaborer avec succès avec les clients pour dépasser leurs objectifs grâce à des conceptions innovantes qui transcendent l'ordinaire.

Son utilisation audacieuse de la couleur, l'attention qu'elle porte aux détails de conception et son dévouement à l'artisanat donnent lieu à des projets résolument modernes, mais chaleureux et accueillants. L'utilisation de matériaux naturels, tels que le bois et la pierre, confère une sensation tactile aux conceptions de la TCA, et l'attention portée à l'expérience de l'utilisateur garantit que les bâtiments de la TCA sont des lieux où les gens se sentent bienvenus et confortables.

Bill Curran, director y fundador de TCA Architects, es un diseñador consumado. Su enfoque práctico y proactivo garantiza que los objetivos de diseño y los estándares de calidad se mantengan en todo el trabajo de la empresa.

El agudo sentido del diseño de Bill guía todos los proyectos de TCA. Su capacidad para observar, comunicar y, sobre todo, escuchar, le ha permitido colaborar con éxito con los clientes para superar sus objetivos con diseños innovadores que trascienden lo ordinario.

Su audaz uso del color, su atención a los detalles del diseño y su dedicación a la artesanía dan como resultado proyectos decididamente modernos, pero a la vez cálidos y acogedores. Su uso de materiales naturales, como la madera y la piedra, confiere tacto a los diseños de TCA, y su atención a la experiencia del usuario garantiza que los edificios de TCA sean lugares en los que la gente se sienta bienvenida y cómoda.

Located in the heart of Niagara wine country, this modest but high quality retail and tasting pavilion is placed amongst the vines to create an authentic vineyard experience for visitors. The building's simple but striking wedge shape is derived from the design of local agricultural buildings and sheds, and the exterior is clad in distinctive Japanese 'Shou Sugi Ban' charred cedar with natural accents. A glass cube at the end of the building offers panoramic views into the vineyard and functions as a private tasting room. The main space is oriented to the vines and has a long marble tasting bar, and carefully designed displays and shelving to animate the simple interior. A plywood strip ceiling is an inexpensive option to timber. The architect's discerning use of colour, attention to detail in design and dedication to craft result in a building that is decidedly modern, but still warm and inviting.

Situé au cœur de la région viticole de Niagara, ce pavillon de vente et de dégustation est installé parmi les vignes afin de créer une expérience authentique du vignoble pour les visiteurs. La forme cunéiforme simple mais frappante du bâtiment s'inspire de la conception des bâtiments agricoles et des hangars locaux, et l'extérieur est revêtu de cèdre calciné japonais «Shou Sugi Ban» aux détails naturels. Un cube de verre situé à l'extrémité du bâtiment offre une vue panoramique sur le vignoble et fait office de salle de dégustation privée. L'espace principal fait face aux vignes et comporte un long bar de dégustation en marbre, ainsi que des présentoirs et des étagères soigneusement conçus. Un plafond à lattes en contreplaqué est un choix économique par rapport au bois. L'utilisation rigoureuse de la couleur par l'architecte, l'attention portée aux détails de la conception et le dévouement à l'artisanat ont donné naissance à un bâtiment résolument moderne, mais chaleureux et accueillant.

Dieser Verkaufs- und Verkostungspavillon befindet sich im Herzen des Niagara-Weinlandes und ist inmitten der Reben platziert, um ein authentisches Weinbergserlebnis für Besucher zu schaffen. Die schlichte, aber markante Keilform des Gebäudes ist inspiriert vom Design lokaler Bauernhöfe und Schuppen. Die Außenverkleidung besteht aus der charakteristischen japanischen „Shou Sugi Ban"-Zedernholzverkleidung mit natürlichen Details. Ein Glaskubus am Ende des Gebäudes bietet einen Panoramablick auf den Weinberg und fungiert als privater Verkostungsraum. Der Hauptraum ist den Weinbergen zugewandt und verfügt über eine lange Verkostungstheke aus Marmor sowie sorgfältig gestaltete Auslagen und Regale, die das schlichte Interieur beleben. Eine Lattenrostdecke aus Sperrholz ist eine wirtschaftliche Alternative zu Holz. Der anspruchsvolle Umgang des Architekten mit Farben, die Liebe zum Detail im Design und die Hingabe zur Handwerkskunst resultieren in einem Gebäude, das entschieden modern, aber dennoch warm und einladend ist.

Situado en el corazón de la región vinícola de Niágara, este pabellón de venta y degustación está situado entre las viñas para crear una auténtica experiencia de viñedo para los visitantes. La sencilla pero llamativa forma de cuña del edificio se inspira en el diseño de los edificios y cobertizos agrícolas locales, y el exterior está revestido con el característico cedro carbonizado japonés "Shou Sugi Ban" con detalles naturales. Un cubo de cristal en el extremo del edificio ofrece vistas panorámicas del viñedo y funciona como sala de degustación privada. El espacio principal está orientado a las viñas y cuenta con una larga barra de degustación de mármol, así como con expositores y estanterías cuidadosamente diseñados. Un techo de listones de madera contrachapada es una opción económica a la madera. Se trata de un edificio decididamente moderno, pero a la vez cálido y acogedor.

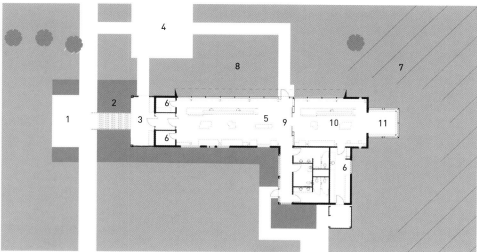

Site plan

1. Forecourt entry
2. Bridge
3. Porch
4. Terrace
5. Fireplace
6. Service / staff
7. Vineyards
8. Future pond
9. Tasting / retail
10. Group tasting / retail
11. Glass cube tasting room

0   10m

N

TZOU

TZOU LUBROTH ARCHITEKTEN

WWW.TZOULUBROTH.COM

> **HM LANG WINE PRESS**

Tzou Lubroth Architekten is an award-winning architectural practice based in Vienna, Austria. Our practice is built on the belief that architecture is a social act, part of a process by which desires are materialized causing environments to change. We believe that architecture only gains relevance through an open dialog. Each of our projects is influenced by the qualities of individual places and by the people that inhabit them. While the outcome of our work may vary widely in shape or form, our design process remains sensitive to a context and to the desires that promise to change it.

We are interested in people and their communities. Understanding and questioning how we work, play, rest, consume, and co-exist is at the heart of our design process.

We are committed to the idea that design can inspire; that it can enrich our lives and affect the way we interact with the world around us.

Tzou Lubroth Architekten ist ein preisgekröntes Architektur-büro mit Sitz in Wien, Österreich. Unser Studio basiert auf der Überzeugung, dass Architektur ein sozialer Akt ist, Teil eines Prozesses, durch den Wünsche materialisiert werden und eine Veränderung der Umwelt bewirken. Wir glauben, dass Architektur nur durch einen offenen Dialog relevant wird. Jedes unserer Projekte wird von den Qualitäten der einzelnen Orte und den Menschen, die sie bewohnen, beeinflusst. Während das Ergebnis unserer Arbeit in der Form stark variieren kann, bleibt unser Designprozess sensibel für einen Kontext und die Wünsche, die ihn zu verändern versprechen.

Wir sind an den Menschen und ihren Gemeinschaften interessiert. Zu verstehen und zu hinterfragen, wie wir arbeiten, spielen, ausruhen, konsumieren und zusammenleben, steht im Mittelpunkt unseres Designprozesses.

Wir sind der Idee verpflichtet, dass Design inspirieren kann; dass es unser Leben bereichern und die Art und Weise beeinflussen kann, wie wir mit der Welt um uns herum interagieren.

LUBROTH ARCHITEKTEN

Tzou Lubroth Architekten est un cabinet d'architectes primé, basé à Vienne, en Autriche. Notre studio est fondé sur la conviction que l'architecture est un acte social, faisant partie d'un processus par lequel les désirs se matérialisent en provoquant des changements dans l'environnement. Nous pensons que l'architecture ne devient pertinente que par le biais d'un dialogue ouvert. Chacun de nos projets est influencé par les qualités des lieux individuels et des personnes qui les habitent. Si le résultat de notre travail peut varier considérablement dans sa forme, notre processus de conception reste sensible à un contexte et aux désirs qui promettent de le changer.

Nous nous intéressons aux personnes et à leurs communautés. Comprendre et remettre en question la façon dont nous travaillons, jouons, nous reposons, consommons et vivons ensemble est au cœur de notre processus de conception.

Nous sommes attachés à l'idée que le design peut inspirer, qu'il peut enrichir nos vies et influer sur la façon dont nous interagissons avec le monde qui nous entoure.

Tzou Lubroth Architekten es un premiado estudio de arquitectura con sede en Viena, Austria. Nuestro estudio se basa en la creencia de que la arquitectura es un acto social, parte de un proceso por el que los deseos se materializan provocando el cambio del entorno. Creemos que la arquitectura sólo adquiere relevancia a través de un diálogo abierto. Cada uno de nuestros proyectos está influenciado por las cualidades de los lugares individuales y por las personas que los habitan. Aunque el resultado de nuestro trabajo puede variar mucho en cuanto a la forma, nuestro proceso de diseño sigue siendo sensible a un contexto y a los deseos que prometen cambiarlo.

Nos interesan las personas y sus comunidades. Entender y cuestionar cómo trabajamos, jugamos, descansamos, consumimos y convivimos es el núcleo de nuestro proceso de diseño.

Estamos comprometidos con la idea de que el diseño puede inspirar; que puede enriquecer nuestras vidas y afectar a la forma en que interactuamos con el mundo que nos rodea.

Mr. & Mrs. Lang are vintners producing exceptional organic wines from their vineyards terraced above the Danube at the beginning of the Wachau valley. The press sits on an old fruit orchard above an old rock-cut tunnel carved out in the early 20th century, which currently houses the wine cellar. This Wine Press puts an ancient pressing principle into modern clothes and technology. The basket lever press applies force through the combination of a long steel lever and a 6-ton weight; an efficient, but at the same time, very gentle pressing process, as the grapes are not moved. The pressed must flows in shallow trenches engraved on the concrete base that lead to a long funnel and lead directly into stainless drums in the wine cellar through a hose that is drilled through the rock, allowing gravity to play an essential part in the process. The mechanical components are covered by a cantilevering, partially louvered roof.

M. et Mme Lang sont des vignerons qui produisent des vins biologiques exceptionnels dans leurs vignobles en terrasses au-dessus du Danube, au début de la vallée de la Wachau. Le pressoir est situé dans un ancien verger, au-dessus d'un ancien tunnel creusé dans la roche au début du XXe siècle, qui abrite aujourd'hui la cave. Ce pressoir met en œuvre un principe de pressage ancien avec des vêtements et une technologie modernes. Le pressoir à levier à panier applique la force par la combinaison d'un long levier en acier et d'un poids de 6 tonnes ; un processus de pressage efficace, mais en même temps très doux, car les raisins ne bougent pas. Le moût pressé s'écoule dans des tranchées peu profondes creusées dans le socle en béton, menant à un long entonnoir, et se déverse directement dans des fûts en acier inoxydable dans la cave par un tuyau percé dans la roche, ce qui permet à la gravité de jouer un rôle essentiel dans le processus. Les composants mécaniques sont couverts par un toit en porte-à-faux, partiellement persienné.

Herr und Frau Lang sind Winzer, die in ihren terrassierten Weingärten oberhalb der Donau am Beginn der Wachau außergewöhnliche Bio-Weine erzeugen. Die Kelterei befindet sich in einem ehemaligen Obstgarten über einem alten, Anfang des 20. Jahrhunderts in den Felsen gegrabenen Tunnel, in dem heute die Weinkellerei untergebracht ist. Diese Weinpresse setzt ein uraltes Pressprinzip mit moderner Kleidung und Technik um. Die Korbhebelpresse übt durch die Kombination eines langen Stahlhebels und eines Gewichts von 6 Tonnen Kraft aus; ein effizienter Pressvorgang, aber gleichzeitig sehr schonend, da sich die Trauben nicht bewegen. Der gepresste Most fließt in flache, in den Betonsockel gehauene Gräben, die zu einem langen Trichter führen, und fließt durch einen in den Fels gebohrten Schlauch direkt in Edelstahlfässer im Keller, so dass die Schwerkraft eine wesentliche Rolle im Prozess spielt. Die mechanischen Komponenten werden durch ein auskragendes, teilweise lamellenartiges Dach abgedeckt.

El Sr. y la Sra. Lang son viticultores que producen excepcionales vinos ecológicos en sus viñedos situados en terrazas sobre el Danubio, al principio del valle de Wachau. El lagar se encuentra en un antiguo huerto frutal sobre un antiguo túnel excavado en la roca a principios del siglo XX, que actualmente alberga la bodega. Este lagar pone en práctica un antiguo principio de prensado con ropa y tecnología modernas. La prensa de palanca de cesta aplica la fuerza mediante la combinación de una larga palanca de acero y un peso de 6 toneladas; un proceso de prensado eficaz, pero al mismo tiempo muy suave, ya que las uvas no se mueven. El mosto prensado fluye en zanjas poco profundas grabadas en la base de hormigón que conducen a un largo embudo y desembocan directamente en bidones de acero inoxidable en la bodega a través de una manguera perforada en la roca, lo que permite que la gravedad desempeñe un papel esencial en el proceso. Los componentes mecánicos están cubiertos por un techo en voladizo, parcialmente apersianado.

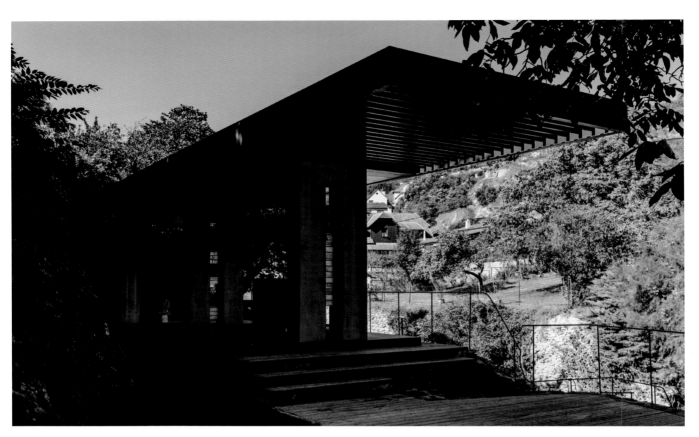

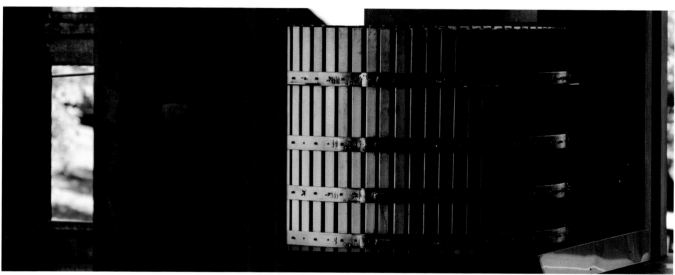

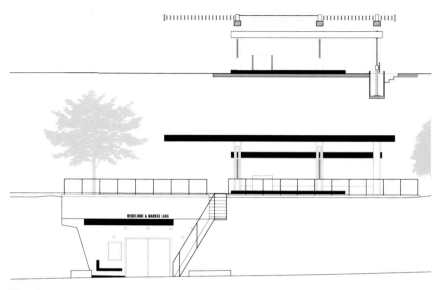

Elevations

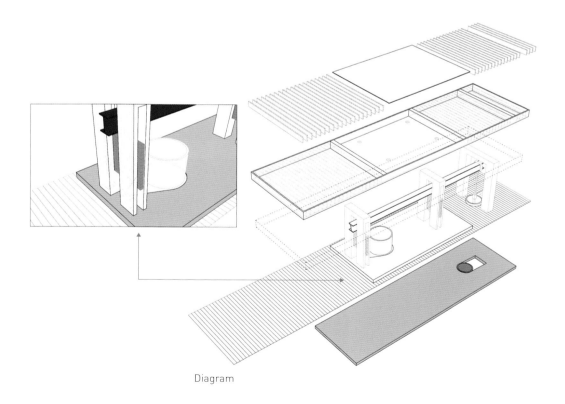

Diagram

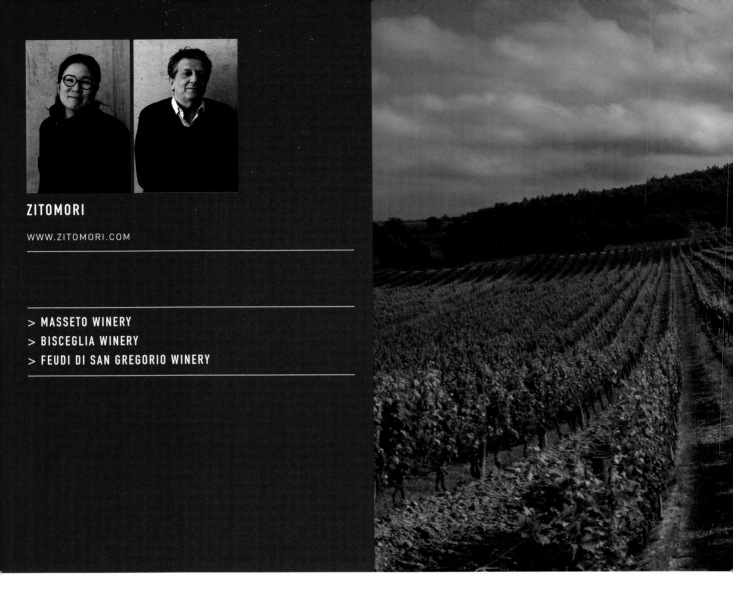

ZITOMORI

WWW.ZITOMORI.COM

> MASSETO WINERY
> BISCEGLIA WINERY
> FEUDI DI SAN GREGORIO WINERY

ZITOMORI is the architecture and design practice founded in 1996 by Hikaru Mari and Maurizio Zito, based in Milan, Italy. The objective of ZITOMORI's work is to give shape to a vision, responding to complex programs at any scale, offering integrated approach to design, architecture, landscape and territory. By considering each project as unique, with its own diversity, through a process of dialogue, research and analysis ZITOMORI reaches the intuition to achieve the specific and tangible design, challenging experimentation in contemporary architecture. Architectural works include Feudi di San Gregario Winery, Bisceglia Winery, Controne city riverside Park, lrpinia Milan Expo Pavillion, Vigna la Corte resort and spa. Renovation and restoration works include: the Mediterranean Local Culture Center (Palazzo Vitale, XVIII century), Venice Biennale Japan Pavillion (with Toyo Ito), SS. Pietá Convent (XV century).

ZITOMORI ist das 1996 von Hikaru Mari und Maurizio Zito gegründete Architektur- und Designstudio mit Sitz in Mailand, Italien. Das Ziel der Arbeit von ZITOMORI ist es, eine Vision zu gestalten, die auf komplexe Programme in jedem Maßstab reagiert und einen integrierten Ansatz für Design, Architektur, Landschaft und Territorium bietet. Indem jedes Projekt als einzigartig betrachtet wird, mit seiner eigenen Vielfalt, durch einen Prozess des Dialogs, der Forschung und der Analyse, erreicht ZITOMORI die Intuition, um spezifisches und greifbares Design zu erreichen, das das Experimentieren in der zeitgenössischen Architektur herausfordert. Zu den architektonischen Arbeiten gehören die Weinkeller Feudi di San Gregario, die Weinkeller Bisceglia, der Park am Flussufer in der Stadt Controne, der Pavillon für die Expo Milano Irpinia, der Touristenkomplex und das Thermalbad Vigna la Corte. Zu den Renovierungs- und Restaurierungsarbeiten gehören: das lokale Kulturzentrum des Mittelmeers (Palazzo Vitale, 18. Jahrhundert), der Japan-Pavillon der Biennale von Venedig (mit Toyo Ito), das Kloster SS. Pietà (15. Jahrhundert).

ZITOMORI

ZITOMORI est le studio d'architecture et de design fondé en 1996 par Hikaru Mari et Maurizio Zito, basé à Milan, en Italie. L'objectif du travail de ZITOMORI est de façonner une vision, en répondant à des programmes complexes à n'importe quelle échelle, offrant une approche intégrée du design, de l'architecture, du paysage et du territoire. En considérant chaque projet comme unique, avec sa propre diversité, à travers un processus de dialogue, de recherche et d'analyse, ZITOMORI atteint l'intuition de réaliser un design spécifique et tangible, défiant l'expérimentation dans l'architecture contemporaine. Parmi les œuvres architecturales, citons les caves Feudi di San Gregario, les caves Bisceglia, le parc fluvial de la ville de Controne, le pavillon de l'Expo Milano Irpinia, le complexe touristique et les thermes de Vigna la Corte. Parmi les travaux de rénovation et de restauration, citons : le centre culturel local de la Méditerranée (Palazzo Vitale, XVIIIe siècle), le pavillon japonais de la Biennale de Venise (avec Toyo Ito), le couvent SS. Pietà (XVe siècle).

ZITOMORI es el estudio de arquitectura y diseño fundado en 1996 por Hikaru Mari y Maurizio Zito, con sede en Milán, Italia. El objetivo del trabajo de ZITOMORI es dar forma a una visión, respondiendo a programas complejos a cualquier escala, ofreciendo un enfoque integrado del diseño, la arquitectura, el paisaje y el territorio. Al considerar cada proyecto como único, con su propia diversidad, a través de un proceso de diálogo, investigación y análisis, ZITOMORI alcanza la intuición para lograr el diseño específico y tangible, desafiando la experimentación en la arquitectura contemporánea. Entre las obras arquitectónicas destacan las bodegas Feudi di San Gregario, las bodegas Bisceglia, el parque ribereño de la ciudad de Controne, el pabellón de la Expo de Milán Irpinia, el complejo turístico y el spa Vigna la Corte. Las obras de renovación y restauración incluyen: el Centro Cultural Local del Mediterráneo (Palazzo Vitale, siglo XVIII), el Pabellón de Japón de la Bienal de Venecia (con Toyo Ito), el Convento SS. Pietà (siglo XV).

We extracted the concept by visiting the site to know its territory and the philosophy: the quarry. It's a tribute to a worksite and also to the wider history of human effort and its interaction with the environment. This concept led us to create an inner architecture, visible only from inside. The surfaces are the boundaries linking the void (internal space) to a surrounding mas (infinity). The space is obtained from extraction, rather than construction. This very individual concept offers a shape to a vision for the winery, responding to reinforce the brand's identity.

Nous avons extrait le concept en visitant le lieu pour connaître son territoire et sa philosophie : la carrière. Il s'agit d'un hommage à un lieu de travail, mais aussi à l'histoire plus large de l'activité humaine et de son interaction avec l'environnement. Ce concept nous a conduit à créer une architecture intérieure, visible uniquement de l'intérieur. Les surfaces sont les frontières qui relient le vide (espace intérieur) à la masse environnante (infini). L'espace est obtenu par extraction plutôt que par construction. Ce concept très individuel offre une vision pour la cave, renforçant l'identité de la marque.

Wir haben das Konzept extrahiert, indem wir den Ort besucht haben, um sein Territorium und seine Philosophie kennenzulernen: den Steinbruch. Es ist eine Hommage an einen Arbeitsplatz und auch an die breitere Geschichte menschlicher Bestrebungen und ihrer Interaktion mit der Umwelt. Dieses Konzept führte uns zu einer Innenarchitektur, die nur von innen sichtbar ist. Die Flächen sind die Grenzen, die die Leere (Innenraum) mit der umgebenden Masse (Unendlichkeit) verbinden. Der Raum wird durch Extraktion und nicht durch Konstruktion gewonnen. Dieses sehr individuelle Konzept bietet eine Vision für das Weingut und stärkt die Markenidentität.

Extrajimos el concepto visitando el lugar para conocer su territorio y la filosofía: la cantera. Es un homenaje a un lugar de trabajo y también a la historia más amplia del esfuerzo humano y su interacción con el entorno. Este concepto nos llevó a crear una arquitectura interior, visible sólo desde dentro. Las superficies son los límites que unen el vacío (espacio interior) con la masa circundante (infinito). El espacio se obtiene a partir de la extracción, más que de la construcción. Este concepto tan individual ofrece una visión para la bodega, reforzando la identidad de la marca.

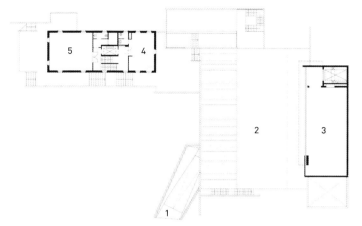

Plan level +1

1. Visitors entrance
2. Grapes reception area
3. Grapes reception building
4. Service room
5. Tasting room

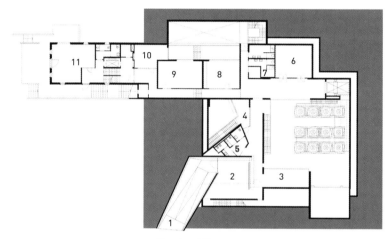

Plan level 0

1. Visitors entrance
2. Reception hall
3. Gallery fermentation tanksroom
4. Visit entrance
5. Visitors restrooms
6. Storage
7. Locker room
8. Cellar office
9. Office
10. Canteen
11. Tasting room

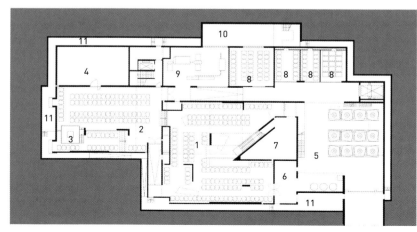

Plan level -1

1. 1 year barrels room
2. 2 years barrels room
3. Tasting room
4. Wine library
5. Fermentation tanksroom
6. Barrel washing
7. Storage
8. Final aging barrel room
9. Blending and bottling room
10. External corridor
11. Service corridor

N

The winery winds in a series of different atmospheres. Going into the building we find an entrance hall in a central position and on its left the productive area, a bottleling space with a large opening towards the archaeological site outside, a clear and clean place. This is a double heighten room controlled by the lab placed on a glass and steel structure, very important in the creation of the product, wich, representing a very rare situation in wineries, shows itself on the main façade. At the back, but physically connected, takes place the storage area with his own access reserved to commercial delivery. On the right of the productive area we found spaces for visitors, a hall, a big multifunctional space for events, conferences, international and intercultural exchanges, exhibitions, wine bar and an exhibition area/shop selling wines and typical products.

Le domaine viticole serpente à travers une série d'environnements différents. En entrant dans le bâtiment, nous trouvons un hall d'entrée central et, à sa gauche, la zone de production, un espace de mise en bouteille avec une grande ouverture sur le site extérieur, un endroit clair et propre. Il s'agit d'une salle à double hauteur contrôlée par le laboratoire placé sur une structure de verre et d'acier, très importante dans la création du produit, qui, représentant une situation très rare dans les caves, est présentée sur la façade principale. A l'arrière, mais physiquement connectée, se trouve la zone de stockage avec son propre accès réservé à la livraison commerciale. À droite de la zone de production, nous trouvons des espaces pour les visiteurs, un foyer, un grand espace multifonctionnel pour les événements, les conférences, les échanges internationaux et interculturels, les expositions, un bar à vin et un espace exposition/boutique pour les vins et les produits typiques.

Das Weingut schlängelt sich durch eine Reihe von verschiedenen Umgebungen. Wenn man das Gebäude betritt, findet man eine Eingangshalle in zentraler Lage und links davon den Produktionsbereich, einen Abfüllraum mit einer großen Öffnung zum Außengelände, ein klarer und sauberer Ort. Es handelt sich um einen Raum mit doppelter Höhe, der vom Labor kontrolliert wird, das sich auf einer Struktur aus Glas und Stahl befindet, die für die Herstellung des Produkts sehr wichtig ist und die, was eine sehr seltene Situation in Weinkellereien darstellt, an der Hauptfassade zu sehen ist. Auf der Rückseite, aber physisch verbunden, befindet sich der Lagerbereich mit einem eigenen Zugang, der für die kommerzielle Anlieferung reserviert ist. Rechts vom Produktionsbereich befinden sich Räume für Besucher, ein Foyer, ein großer multifunktionaler Raum für Veranstaltungen, Konferenzen, internationalen und interkulturellen Austausch, Ausstellungen, Weinbar und ein Ausstellungs-/Ladenbereich für Weine und typische Produkte.

La bodega serpentea en una serie de ambientes diferentes. Adentrándonos en el edificio encontramos un hall de entrada en posición central y a su izquierda la zona productiva, un espacio de embotellado con una gran apertura hacia el yacimiento exterior, un lugar claro y limpio. Se trata de una sala de doble altura controlada por el laboratorio colocado sobre una estructura de vidrio y acero, muy importante en la creación del producto, que, representando una situación muy rara en las bodegas, se muestra en la fachada principal. En la parte posterior, pero físicamente conectada, se sitúa la zona de almacenamiento con su propio acceso reservado a la entrega comercial. A la derecha de la zona productiva encontramos espacios para visitantes, un vestíbulo, un gran espacio multifuncional para eventos, conferencias, intercambios internacionales e interculturales, exposiciones, bar de vinos y una zona de exposición/tienda de vinos y productos típicos.

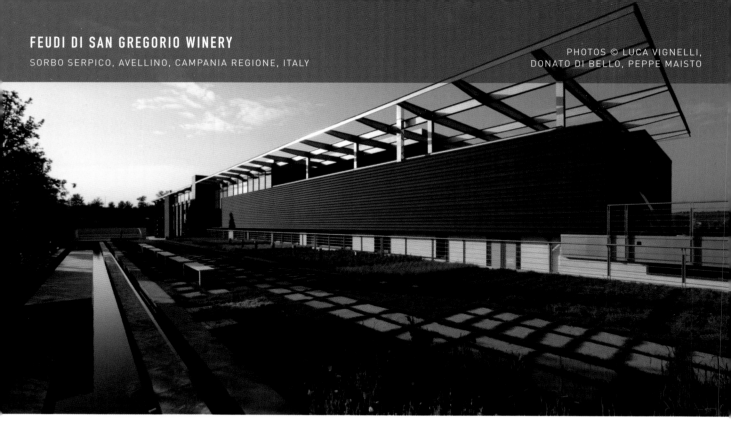

Spaces and functions were designed with a unique philosophy in the different areas of the winery (production, delivery, administration, marketing, visitors spaces with shop and wine tasting areas...). All the functions were designed in order to be physically separated, but at the same time functionally connected.

The intervention is an answer to the ambitious intention of the Feudi di San Gregorio winery, building a winery that could be a forum, a meeting place, of comparison, of knowledge, of meditation, a laboratory of ideas and culture. The result is an organic intervention integrated with the territory and the landscape, a structure that, due to the functions and activities for which it was designed, is developed mainly underground, integrating to the landscape and the geography of the place.

Les espaces et les fonctions ont été conçus avec une philosophie unique dans les différents domaines de la cave (production, livraison, administration, marketing, espaces visiteurs avec boutique et zones de dégustation...). Toutes les fonctions ont été conçues pour être physiquement séparées, mais en même temps fonctionnellement connectées.

L'intervention répond à l'intention ambitieuse de la cave Feudi di San Gregorio de construire un espace qui serait un forum, un lieu de rencontre, de comparaison, de connaissance, de méditation, un laboratoire d'idées et de culture. Le résultat est une intervention organique intégrée au territoire et au paysage, une structure qui, en raison des fonctions et des activités pour lesquelles elle a été conçue, se développe principalement en sous-sol, s'intégrant au paysage et à la géographie du lieu.

Räume und Funktionen wurden mit einer einzigartigen Philosophie in den verschiedenen Bereichen des Weingutes (Produktion, Auslieferung, Verwaltung, Marketing, Besucherräume mit Shop und Verkostungsbereichen...) gestaltet. Alle Funktionen wurden so konzipiert, dass sie physikalisch getrennt, aber gleichzeitig funktional verbunden sind.

Der Eingriff entspricht der ehrgeizigen Absicht des Weinguts Feudi di San Gregorio, einen Raum zu bauen, der ein Forum, ein Ort der Begegnung, des Vergleichs, des Wissens, der Meditation, ein Laboratorium der Ideen und der Kultur sein sollte. Das Ergebnis ist ein organischer Eingriff, der mit dem Territorium und der Landschaft integriert ist, eine Struktur, die sich aufgrund der Funktionen und Aktivitäten, für die sie entworfen wurde, hauptsächlich unterirdisch entwickelt und sich mit der Landschaft und der Geographie des Ortes integriert.

Se diseñaron espacios y funciones con una filosofía única en las diferentes áreas de la bodega (producción, entrega, administración, marketing, espacios para visitantes con tienda y zonas de cata de vinos...). Todas las funciones se diseñaron para estar físicamente separadas, pero al mismo tiempo funcionalmente conectadas.

La intervención responde a la ambiciosa intención de la bodega Feudi di San Gregorio de construir un espacio que fuera un foro, un lugar de encuentro, de comparación, de conocimiento, de meditación, un laboratorio de ideas y de cultura. El resultado es una intervención orgánica integrada con el territorio y el paisaje, una estructura que, debido a las funciones y actividades para las que fue diseñada, se desarrolla principalmente bajo tierra, integrándose al paisaje y a la geografía del lugar.

ARDESHIR NOZARI + ROSHAN NOZARI ARCHITECTS
DARIOUSH WINERY

PHOTO © SARA MOYNIER

DIRECTORY

2B&G (BELLIA-BOMBARA-GIANNETTO INGEGNERI) + AMORE CAMPIONE ARCHITETTURA
www.studioaca.com

CANTINA GRACI
Location: Passopisciaro, Catania, Italy
Client: Az. Agr. GRACI
Creator, Designer and Director
of Works: Studio 2B&G:
ing. Cettino Bellia, Ing. Maria Bombara,
ing. Giannetto Carmelo Antonio
Architect and Artist direction: ACA Amore
Campione Architettura: arch. Sebastiano
Amore, ing. Angela Campione
Contractor: Campione s.r.l.
Photos: Sebastiano Amore
Aerial overview: Benedetto Tarantino

ALESSANDRO ISOLA STUDIO
www.alessandroisola.com

LE MONDE WINERY. WINE TASTING ROOM / OUTDOOR SPACE
Location: Prata di Pordenone, Italy
Photos: Studio Auber

ALLIED WORKS
www.alliedworks.com

SOKOL BLOSSER WINERY PAVILION
Location: Dayton, Oregon, USA
Lead Designer: Brad Cloepfil
Principal-in-Charge: Kyle Lommen
Project Manager: John Weil
Project Architect: Nathan Hamilton
Project Team: Kathryn van Voorhees,
Christopher Brown, Scott Miller,
Jared Abraham, Brent Linden, Emily Kappes,
Sushwala Hedding, Neal Harrod
Structural Engineering: KPFF
Building Systems Engineering: Glumac
Sustainability: Green Building Services
Horticulture: Tom Fischer
Promoter: Sokol Blosser Winery
Builder: R & H Construction
Area: 530 m^2
Photos: Jeremy Bittermann / JBSA
Aerial overview: Skyris Imaging

ANDREAS BURGHARDT
www.burghardt.co.at

FRED LOIMER
Location: Langenlois, Austria
Photos: Andreas Burghardt

NEUMEISTER WEINGUT
Location: Straden, Austria
Photos: Andreas Burghardt

NIEPOORT WINERY
Location: Douro Valley, Portugal
Photos: Rita Burmeester

ARCHINGEGNO
www.archingegno.info

CANTINA VALETTI
Location: Bardolino, Verona, Italy
Client: Azienda Vinicola Valetti Luigi
Project Architect: Carlo Ferrari,
Alberto Pontiroli
Project Team: Andrea Chelidonio,
Alessandro Martini, Francesca Rapisarda,
Marco Rizzi, Giovanni Montresor,
Mattia Gaspari, Massimo Padovan,
Davide Piacentini, Luca Bonato
Photos: Alessandra Chemollo

ARDESHIR NOZARI + ROSHAN NOZARI ARCHITECTS

www.nozariarchitects.com

DARIOUSH WINERY

Location: Napa, California, USA
Clients: Darioush and Shahpar Khaledi
Program: Winery and Residence
Architectural Design Team: Ardeshir Nozari,
Roshan Ghaffarian Nozari, Julie Herrera,
Interior Design Team: Roshan Ghaffarian
Nozari, Shahpar Khaledi, Ardeshir Nozari,
Julie Herrera
Construction Management: Ardeshir Nozari
Structural Engineer: Mansour Namdar
Landscape Architect: Proscape Landscape
Design
Contractor: James Nolan Construction
Area: 2,044 m²
Photos: Timothy Street Porter,
Ardeshir Nozari, Sara Moynier,
Doug Sterling, Randall Cordero,
Frederic Lagrange, Craig Lee,
Ali Matin Photography
Photo Compilation: Alessandra Murillo,
Kimia Nozari, Roxane Ghaffarian
Aerial overview: Chris Straughn

BC ESTUDIO ARCHITECTS. JAVIER BARBA

www.bcestudioarchitects.com

WAULTRAUD CELLAR FOR BODEGAS TORRES

Location: Vilafranca del Penedés, Barcelona,
Spain
Lead architect: Javier Barba
Architects: Susana Zanón, Jordi Barba,
Gabriel Barba
Photos: Jordi Elias

VISITOR CENTER, STAG'S LEAP WINE CELLAR WINERY

Location: Napa Valley, California, USA
Lead architect: Javier Barba
Architects: Susana Zanón, Jordi Barba,
Gabriel Barba
Photos: Pamela Platt

STAG'S LEAP WINE CELLARS

Location: Napa Valley, California, USA
Lead architect: Javier Barba
Architects: Susana Zanón, Jordi Barba,
Gabriel Barba
Photos: Pamela Platt

DELL'AGNOLO - KELDERER ARCHITEKTURBÜRO

www.da-k.net

KELLEREI BOZEN WINERY

Location: Bozen, Südtirol, Italy
Client: Cantina Produttori Bolzano Soc. Coop.
Planners: Dell'Agnolo Kelderer
Architekturbüro (Dr. Arch Sylvia Dell'Agnolo,
Dr. Ing. Egon Kelderer)
Structures: Ingenieurbüro Pohl+Partner GmbH
Artistic direction: Dell'Agnolo Kelderer
Architekturbüro
Facilities (electric, heating and cooling
systems): Ingenieurbüro Dr. Fleischmann &
Dr. Janser
Construction Management: Baubüro
Ingenieurgemeinschaft
Project management of the facilities:
Ingenieurbüro Dr. Fleischmann & Dr. Janser
Construction Period: 2008 – 2018
Awards: CasaClima Awards 2019
Photos: Oskar Da Riz

DESTILAT

www.destilat.at

CLEMENS STROBL WINERY

Location: Mitterstockstall am Wagram,
Austria
Client: Weinmanufaktur Clemens Strobl
Team: Harald Hatschenberger, Sophie
Kessler, Henning Weimer, Agnes Jetzinger,
Lukasz Paginowski, Magdalena Haas
Executing architects: DI Claus Ullrich
Photos: Monika Nguyen

DVA ARHITEKTA

www.dva-arhitekta.hr

WINERY IN KUTJEVO

Location: Kutjevo, Croatia
Client: Galić Vina
Project architect: Tomislav Ćurković,
Zoran Zidarić
Lead architect: Maja Maroši Pezo
Project team: Mario Pervić
Visualisations: Dejan Šparovec
Photos: Damir Fabijanić

IDOM

www.idom.com

BODEGA BERONIA RIOJA

Location: Ollauri, La Rioja, Spain
Client: Bodegas Beronia, S.A.
Project architects: Borja Gómez,
Gonzalo Tello
Other architects: Manuel Bouzas,
Fernando Garrido, Gonzalo Peñalba,
Andreia Faley
Technical Architect: Juan Dávila
Structures: Carlos Castañón,

Romina González, Jorge de Prado,
Borja Olivares, Beatriz Suárez
Environmental Engineering: Antonio
Villanueva, Isaac Lorenzo, Javier Martín
Electrical Engineering: Carlos Trujillano,
Federico Reguero
Fire: Héctor Mayordomo
Production: Federico Reguero,
Almudena García Bacarizo, Sergio González
Photos: Francesco Pintón, Manuel Bouzas

BODEGA BERONIA RUEDA
Location: Rueda, Valladolid, Spain
Client: Bodegas Beronia, S.A.
Project architects: Gonzalo Tello,
Borja Gómez
Other architects: Andreia Faley,
Carlos Sambricio
Agricultural Engineer: Almudena García
Bacarizo
Project Management: Gonzalo Tello
Costs: Victoria Blázquez
Structures: David García, Jorge de Prado,
Beatriz Suárez
Environmental Engineering: Federico
Reguero, Naiara Moreno, Alejandro Viu
Lighting: Noemí Barbero
Public Health Services: Gorka Viguri
Electrical Engineering: Elena Guezuraga
Process Facilities: Federico Reguero
Site Supervision: Gonzalo Tello
Construction execution management:
María Victoria Blázquez
Photos: Aitor Ortiz

INMAT ARQUITECTURA
www.inmat.es

CEHEGÍN WINE SCHOOL
Location: Cehegín, Murcia, Spain
Owner: Cehegín City Hall, Project financed
by Funds FEADER, Comunidad Autónoma de
la Región de Murcia y Excmo. Ayuntamiento
de Cehegín
Area: 342.75 m²
Project Architect: José Luis López Ibáñez
Architecture Project Team: José Luis López

Ibáñez, José Maria Mariñoso Pascual,
David Martínez Ponce, Virginia García Tormo,
Maria José García Morales
Project Manager: José Luis López Ibáñez
Architect, project management: Pablo García
Mora (MOHOARQUITECTOS)
Municipal Technical Architect: Santos Pedro
Guillamón Marcos
Archaeologist and Director of the Municipal
Archaeological Museum: Francisco Manuel
Peñalver Aroca
Photos: David Frutos

KAUNITZ YEUNG ARCHITECTURE
www.kaunitzyeung.com

RUNNING HORSE WINES
Location: Broke, New South Wales, Australia
Photos: Brett Boardman Photography

MARKUS SCHERER
www.architektscherer.it

DAS WEINDORF NALS
Location: Nals, Bolzano, Italy
Photos: Oliver Jaist, Bruno Klomfar,
Helmuth Rier

MARTA GONZÁLEZ ARQUITECTOS
www.martagonzalez.com

BODEGAS PANIZA
Location: Zaragoza, Spain
Project Team: Alejandro Bolado,
Jorge Ferreiro, Eva Rodríguez,
Luis Miguel Gutiérrez.
Area: 3,000 m²
Photos: Rubén Alonso Ramiro

NS STUDIO ARCHITECTURE & DESIGN
www.nsstudio.ge

HOUSE AND WINERY IN ARTANA
Location: Village Artana, Kakheti Region,
Georgia
Project Team: Nino Tchanturia,
Luka Chaganava
Brands used: Nemo, Midj, Ton, Gubi, Aparaci
Area: 400 m² (house), 450 m² (cellar)
Photos: Nick Paniashvili

RESTAURANT ADRE
Location: Tbilisi, Georgia
Project Team: Nino Tchanturia,
Luka Chaganava, Vakhtang Tskhovrebashvili,
Amiran Shariphashvili
Brands used: Nemo, Ton, Grok lighting,
Leds c4, Pedrali
Area: 850 m²
Photos: Nick Paniashvili

VINERIA
Location: Tbilisi, Georgia
Project Team: Nino Tchanturia,
Luka Chaganava, Amiran Shariphashvili
Brands used: Riva 1920, Capdell, Foscarini,
Moroso, Andrew world, David Groppi,
Saba Italia, Leds c4, Grok
Area: 620 m²
Photos: Nick Paniashvili

PLANT. ATELIER PÉTER KIS

www.plant.co.hu

GRAND TOKAJ WINERY

Location: Tolcsva, Hungary
Chief architects: PLANT Atelier Péter Kis:
Péter Kis; Öt Elem: Ákos Dobrányi
Architects: PLANT Atelier Péter Kis:
Tamás Bene, Bea Molnár; Öt Elem: Tamás
Romhányi
Area: 3,800 m²
Year of construction: 2016
Photos: Zsolt Batár

VILLA PÁTZAY WINE ESTATE

Location: Badacsonytomaj, Hungary
Chief architects: Péter Kis, Bea Molnár
Landscape designer: Zsuzsanna Bogner
Area: 820 m²
Year of construction: 2010
Photos: Zsolt Batár

PORTO ARCHITECTS

www.portoarchitects.com

PORTUGAL VINEYARDS CONCEPT STORE

Location: Porto, Portugal
Architect: Ricardo Porto Ferreira
Area: 90 m²
Client: Portugal Vineyards
Photos: Ivo Tavares Studio

RSAAW | RAFAEL SANTA ANA ARCHITECTURE WORKSHOP

www.rsaaw.com

COPPER SPIRIT DISTILLERY

Location: Bowen Island, British Columbia,
Canada
Design: Rafael Santa Ana, Antonio Colin,
Larissa Llevadot, Vicente Castañón-Rumebe
Client: Copper Spirit Distillery
Structural engineers: Aspect Structural
Engineers
Mechanical engineers: Zoom Engineering Ltd
Electrical engineers: Zoom Engineering Ltd
Code consulting: GHL consultants
Contracting: West Coast Turn Key
Gross Built Area: 819 m²
Photos: Andrew Latreille

SEVERIN PROEKT

www.severinproekt.ru

COTE ROCHEUSE WINERY

Location: Varvarovka Village, Anapa,
Krasnodar Region, Russia
Leading architect, author: Alexander Balabin
Chief architect: Elena Vvedenskaya
Chief interior designer: Elena Panferova
Chief engineer: Alexey Nazemnov
Chief project engineer: Vladimir Sadovnikov
Chief constructor: Yarislav Yudin
Leading constructor: Yaroslav Mirnichenko
Chief architect: Nina Ilyina
Managing BIM specialist: Dmitry Prudnikov
Chief designer-visual artist: Dmitry
Baraboshkin
Visual artist: Vladimir Shlennikov
Gross Built Area: 9,752 m²
Photos: Daniel Annenkov

SRTA. ROTTENMEIER

www.srtarottenmeier.com

BODEGA CASA ROJO

Location: Murcia, Spain
Client: Casa Rojo Bodega y Viñedos
Engineers: PGA
Area: 3,700 m²
Ceramic façade: Frontek
Cladding: Porcelanosa, Rocersa
Lighting: Simón y Modular
Alumimnium carpentry: Metra y K-Line
Lift: Otis
Photos: David Frutos

BODEGA VIRGEN DE LAS VIÑAS

Location: Tomelloso, Ciudad Real, Spain
Client: Virgen de las Viñas
Engineers: PGA
Area: 700 m²
Lighting: Lledó
Ceiling: Lledó
Continuous flooring: Pandomo de Ardex
Bath equipment and coverings: Porcelanosa
Photos: Gemma González

SUPERIMPOSE

www.superimpose.nl

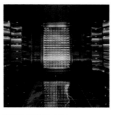

SKY CELLAR

Location: Beijing, China
Client: Beijing SAJC Investment
Management Co., Ltd.
Design team: Carolyn Leung, Ben de Lange,
Ruben Bergambagt, Huimin Xie, Yujia Deng,
Xiaoyu Xu, Casper Kraai
Area: 203 m²
Photos: Marc Goodwin, Superimpose

TCA | THEIR + CURRAN ARCHITECTS

www.tcarch.ca

LAKEVIEW WINE CO. RETAIL & TASTING PAVILION

Location: Niagara-on-the-Lake, Ontario, USA
Lead Architects: Bill Curran, Kyle Slote
Gross Built Area: 261 m²
Photos: Doublespace Photography

TZOU LUBROTH ARCHITEKTEN

www.tzoulubroth.com

HM LANG WINE PRESS

Location: Stein an der Donau, Austria
Architects: Tzou Lubroth Architekten
Design Team: Gregorio S. Lubroth, Chieh-shu Tzou, Lea Artner
Client: Heidelinde & Markus Lang
Total Floor Area: 50 m²
Site Area: 600 m²
Photos: Bengt Stiller

ZITOMORI

www.zitomori.com

MASSETO WINERY

Location: Castagneto Carducci - Fraz. Bolgheri, Livorno, Italy
Client: Ornellaia e Masseto Soc. Agricola srl
Design: Hikaru Mori, Maurizio Zito (ZITOMORI)
Collaborators: Enrico Prato, Angela Abbruzzese, (ZITOMORI)
Structure engineer: Maurizio Ghillani
Merchanical Engeneer: Nicola Martinuzzi
Electrical Engeneer: Yuri Demi
Construction Manager: Maurizio Ghillani
Construction Superviser: Hikaru Mori, Maurizio Zito (ZITOMORI)
Constructor: Target Costruzioni srl
Enological machinery supplier: Pandolfini srl
Custum made interior fixture: RRRetail srl
RC Tanks: Nico Velo spa
Site area: 7,000 m²
Floor space: 2,530 m² (1,560 m² underground)
Photos: Andrea Martiradonna

BISCEGLIA WINERY

Location: Lavello, Potenza, Italy
Project: Hikaru Mori with Maurizio Zito and Domenico Santomauro
Collaborators: Laura Molendini, Davide Pasquariello
Construction manager: Domenico Santomauro, Hikaru Mori
Constructor: Favullo Costruzioni srl
Marbles and stones: Pibamarmi srl
Electrical system: Simm srl
Water system: Tecnoimpianti srl
Air conditioning: Garg srl
Audio: Firefly snc
Fastenings: Cosmai Infissi di Cosmai Francesco
Client: Azienda Agricola Bisceglia srl
Area: 17,500 m² total / 1,400 m² built

FEUDI DI SAN GREGORIO WINERY

Location: Sorbo Serpico, Avellino, Campania Regione, Italy
Client: Feudi di San Gregorio Azienda Agricola SpA
Design: Hikaru Mori with Maurizio Zito (ZITOMORI)
Collaborators: Damiano Deiraghi (ZITOMORI), Chiara Rusconi (ZITOMORI), Laura Molendini (ZITOMORI), Davide Pasquariello (ZITOMORI)
Structure engineer: Antonio Capaldo, Mario Gimigliano
Mechanical Engeneer: Martino Cipolletta
Construction manager: Maurizio Zito (ZITOMORI)
Construction Superviser: Hikaru Mori (ZITOMORI)
Constructor: DAR.CO (building work), Monsud (steel framework and External coverings), Gardenia Calcestruzzi (RC structure), Nicola Maisto (Greenery), Europa Finestre (Fastenings), Simm srl (Electrical system, fire alarm system and anti-theft system), Di Venezia, A. Cesa (IMechanical system), Enoconsult srl (Enological machinery)
Site Area: 27,000 m²
Photos: Luca Vignelli, Donato Di Bello, Peppe Maisto